More Work in Progress

Teacher's Resource Book

Madeleine du Vivier

with Andy Hopkins
and Jocelyn Potter

LONGMAN

Addison Wesley Longman Limited,
Edinburgh Gate, Harlow,
Essex CM20 2JE, England
and Associated Companies throughout the world.

© Addison Wesley Longman Limited 1998

The right of Madeleine du Vivier to be identified as author of this work
has been asserted by her in accordance with the Copyright, Designs and
Patents Act 1988.

ISBN 0 582 27834 1

First Published in 1998

Set in Kuenstler 9pt
Printed in Spain by Gráficas Estella

Typeset by Linemead, UK
Artwork by Kathy Baxendale

Contents

Introduction to the course

More Work in Progress provides a general introduction to English in the world of work. It recognises that people change jobs and move between sectors regularly, but that many of the tasks they have to perform in English in different sectors are broadly similar. They may, for example, need to meet visitors and deal with their queries, handle telephone calls, or understand and send faxes, letters, e-mail messages and other forms of correspondence.

Who is the course for?

This is a course for people who are already working, or who wish to work, in a company in their own country or abroad, where there is a need for a certain amount of English communication. The characters and companies presented in the units illustrate how these needs occur in the context of real people going about their daily work.

More Work in Progress is the second level of a two-book series. Both books have been developed after observing real people operating successfully at work in real companies. The language objectives of *Work in Progress* and *More Work in Progress* derive directly from these observations. *Work in Progress* is a fast-track elementary consolidation course leading to lower-intermediate level. *More Work in Progress* is an intermediate-level course.

What beliefs is the course based on?

- There are basic communication skills that are needed by anyone who needs to use English at work.
- These communication skills are best exemplified by presenting real people in real jobs carrying out real tasks.
- Learners want to know what they are learning and why.
- Learners want to be able to measure their own progress and need a sense of achievement.
- Learners need clear communication goals that are achievable.
- Learners need to develop competences in vocabulary, grammar and functional language to carry out communicative tasks successfully.
- Learners need resources to help them continue learning outside the classroom.
- Topics should be interesting, varied, and relevant to learners' current or future lives.
- Teachers want materials that are clear, principled and flexible.

Course Book

This contains sixteen units, divided into four sections of four units each. Each section is based on real companies in different business areas: retail (a small shop in Spain, part of the British W H Smith retail chain), manufacturing (Neuhaus-Mondose, makers of luxury Belgian chocolates), the media (MTV Europe, a television company with its head office in England and regional offices around Europe) and services (Intra, a market communications company based in Sweden, which specialises in promoting companies on the Web). The multi-syllabus

approach provides development in vocabulary, grammar, functional language and communication skills. At the end of each six-page unit is a 'Word file', which lists new words, followed by a two-page grammar practice and reference section covering the new grammar presented in the unit, or one page of grammar and one page of pronunciation work. There are also four pages of learner training material towards the back of the book. The Course Book offers between 80 and 100 hours of classroom-based work.

Grammar

In the main body of the units, learners are asked to focus inductively on a grammar area in context and to work out key features of form and use. An icon ▶▶ p.45 directs the learner to the related practice / reference pages at the end of the unit. Although the unit notes suggest one way of dealing with new grammar, there are many ways in which the grammar focus can be varied according to your preferences and beliefs about learning.

- Take the learners through the inductive activity presented in the unit to see how much they can work out for themselves about form and use. The teacher can then actively 'present' the grammar point and follow this up with practice exercises from the Grammar Backup pages at the end of each unit before moving back to a freer production task suggested in the Course Book or in the teacher's notes. This is a particularly effective method of presentation if the grammar point is completely new. Practice exercises in the Grammar Backup section are also suitable for homework.

- Start with an inductive activity from the unit. Check learners' understanding and refer them to the reference section in the Grammar Backup if necessary. This can be followed by practice exercises and a freer task.

- Many teachers prefer to present a new grammar point themselves before working with materials. This can be followed by an inductive task from the unit to check understanding before moving on to practice exercises and checking with the reference section. You can then move on to a freer task.

- Some teachers and learners feel they want to read about a grammar point first. If so, the reference section in the Grammar Backup is the place to start. Follow this with an inductive task from the unit before checking learners' understanding and moving on to practice exercises and a freer task.

- If you feel that learners have a reasonable grasp of a particular grammar point already, you might like to begin with a freer task to assess their knowledge. You can then, if necessary, explain gaps in their understanding and turn to more guided practice exercises.

Vocabulary

The materials present new words in context and then offer a range of activities in the Course Book and Workbook to check understanding and encourage use. You may wish to introduce new words before a text is read or played, by encouraging prediction or presenting them in a different context.

Speaking

You may wish to supplement the spoken practice activities by introducing parallel tasks that are directly related to the learners' own contexts.

Writing

There is ample scope for adding extension activities that use real companies in the local area. Company brochures and advertising materials can be brought in, and it may be possible to collect real examples of written correspondence in English from colleagues of course participants or friends who work locally. Collaborative writing can be encouraged in class time, so that learners can help and learn from each other; individual, silent writing is best done at home.

Monitoring, giving feedback, checking answers

Listening and reading texts

Encourage learners to check their answers in pairs before whole class checking. This allows learners to see how much they have understood and builds confidence prior to whole class checking. Ask learners to prompt you as you write answers on the board. With listening texts, play the text through again after checking the answers to ensure all the learners understand.

Language focus exercises

Learners can do the exercises individually but, again, encourage them to check their answers in pairs before writing them on the board.

Freer speaking activities

With roleplays and discussions, allow learners to express themselves freely without negative interference concerning language errors. Monitor them as they speak, and after the activity, write important errors on the board and ask learners to explore why they are wrong and correct them. Alternatively, photocopy a limited number of errors and ask learners to try to correct them for homework.

Features of the Course Book

'Action' points

The 'Action' points contain the language and communication aims of each double-page teaching spread. It can be helpful at the beginning of a lesson to use the points to encourage learners to think about what they already know (e.g. Exhibitions). They can also be used for review purposes by asking learners to recall what they have learnt under each action point at the end of a lesson or unit.

Talking points

The 'Talking points' present learners with points of view with which they might disagree. One way of exploiting them in the classroom is to divide the class into two groups. Ask one group to think of arguments in support of the comment and the other to think of arguments against. Then bring the groups back together for a discussion. Other uses include: discussing learners' own experiences in relation to the point; roleplaying

how the situation or monologue might continue; speculating about the person who made the comment.

Phrasebooks

'Phrasebooks' give a summary of the key functional language learners need to fulfil the communicative tasks. Ways of using specific 'Phrasebooks' are included in the unit notes. However, learners will find it useful to make a phrasebook of their own using the headings given. They can then add phrases to their lists as the course develops. An effective revision activity is to write a 'Phrasebook' heading on the board and ask learners to recall as many expressions as possible. Another idea is to write expressions on pieces of paper and ask learners to work in small groups, taking it in turn to use the expressions in short conversations. For quick revision, write a few gapped expressions from the 'Phrasebooks' on the board and ask learners to complete them.

Word files

These appear at the end of each unit and include all new important words introduced in that unit. They can be used for revision purposes by copying the headings onto the board and asking learners to recall words under each heading. Alternatively, give a definition and ask learners to guess the word. As a warmer, write the words on pieces of paper and place them in a class 'word bag'; learners pick words from the bag and ask their partners to use them in sentences and / or give definitions and their partner guesses the word.

Course Book cassettes

These include all the audio material for working with the Course Book. A full tapescript appears at the back of the Course Book and in the Teacher's Resource Book.

Teacher's Resource Book

The Teacher's Resource Book provides: information on principles that lie behind the course; detailed lesson-by-lesson notes; photocopiable tests (one for each four-unit section); photocopiable supplementary task sheets (indicated by an icon **P** **6.1**) and full keys and tapescripts for the Course Book. The teaching notes highlight possible difficulties, particularly those associated with the pronunciation of new vocabulary, and provide lots of extra practice activities. An introduction to the four companies and the individuals featured in the book is also provided as background material.

Workbook

The Workbook contains sixteen units of practice material to consolidate the vocabulary and the spoken and written communication skills presented in the relevant unit of the Course Book. In the centre is a pull-out key with tapescripts. The Workbook can be used by a learner working alone with the Workbook cassettes, or in the classroom with a teacher. Each unit of the Workbook is designed to be used in its entirety at the end of the parallel Course Book unit. There are three focuses in each Workbook unit:

The right word

Based on the unit Word file, the purpose of the exercises on these pages is to consolidate the meaning and uses of new words encountered in the unit. Pronunciation patterns are also highlighted here.

Face to face

This provides revision of key functional language in conversational contexts. Learners are asked to think through ways of interacting with another speaker, then to listen to a cassette, compare their answers and write what they hear. Then they practise the conversation with the cassette.

Put it in writing

This page provides opportunities for extra practice in working with the text types they have encountered in the parallel Course Book unit. Tasks are often open-ended and sample answers are provided in the key.

Workbook cassettes

These contain all the audio material for working with the Workbook: new words for pronunciation practice; texts for listening; stress and intonation activities; partial conversations for interaction with the cassette; source texts related to writing tasks.

Internet links

Most of the companies featured in the book have English-language Web sites, which are a valuable source of additional information about these businesses. The sites can be accessed directly from the Addison Wesley Longman site (http://www.awl-elt.com), which also contains tasks for learners. Learners can also use information from the sites as a basis for short presentations on the company, the completion of a company profile sheet, or for roleplays involving one learner in 'phoning' or faxing the other for information.

Finally ...

Wherever possible, reference should be made to contexts with which learners are familiar, either in the working lives of family and friends, or in their own. Anything that helps to emphasise the relevance and authenticity of the language they are learning through the course materials will increase motivation and the chances of success.

Good luck!

Andy Hopkins & Jocelyn Potter

Introducing the companies

W H Smith

W H Smith is an institution in British high streets – W H Smith Retail sells books, newspapers, magazines, stationery, cards, videos and music in more than 500 shops around the UK. The W H Smith Group also includes, at the time of writing: Virgin Our Price, a chain of specialist shops selling music, video and computer games; Waterstone's, a bookselling chain; W H Smith News, which distributes newspapers and magazines to other retailers; and W H Smith Inc., which runs airport and hotel shops in the United States. There are also W H Smith bookshops in a number of European cities.

The W H Smith shop in Alicante Airport, in eastern Spain, opened in 1995 with Isabel Espinosa as manager and Andrew Thomas as her deputy. It sells a wide range of products, including English-language books and newspapers and souvenirs for tourists. Isabel uses English for phone and fax communication with W H Smith offices and warehouses in Britain (where her boss is based and some of the shop's products come from), and Spanish with local suppliers and airport employees. She and Andrew use the two languages interchangeably when talking to each other. The sales staff are all Spanish, but many of their customers – especially in the summer months – are British visitors or expatriates who hope or expect counter transactions to take place in English. Other foreign tourists may also be more comfortable with English than Spanish. The staff are also routinely asked for help, advice and directions by departing and arriving passengers.

We would like to thank Isabel Espinosa, Andrew Thomas, Raquel Fernández, Carmen Sempere and Nuria Mollà for their help.

Neuhaus-Mondose

Jean Neuhaus left his native Switzerland for Belgium in 1857. In Brussels he opened a pharmacy and confectionery shop with his brother-in-law, a chemist; there he made different kinds of sweets and chocolate bars. His son, Frederick, experimented with sugar and almonds to provide the fillings that his own son, Jean, introduced into empty chocolate shells after he took over in 1912. The family business grew fast, and soon there were a number of Neuhaus shops. It became a company, and now Neuhaus-Mondose (including Neuhaus, Mondose and Jeff de Bruges) is part of a Belgian holding company called Artal. There are Neuhaus shops in Belgium, and in-store boutiques in other countries. Over a hundred varieties of chocolates – manufactured in a plant outside Brussels – are exported around the world.

Karine van Geel is the marketing manager of Neuhaus Mondose. She uses English to talk to buyers, journalists and other visitors to the company, and to write marketing material. She also travels to exhibitions and presentations of Neuhaus products. Sylvia Devogeleer is a product manager. Karin Thielemans is an assistant to the export manager. Eliane van Laethem is a receptionist at the Neuhaus headquarters and secretary to the managing director.

We would like to thank Karine van Geel, Eliane van Laethem, Sylvia Devogeleer, Karin Thielemans, Ann Bobert and Daniel Staellaert for their help.

Introduction

MTV Europe

MTV, a cable television company producing programmes for young people, was launched in 1981 and now serves hundreds of millions of households around the world. Much of its programming is in English, but it also broadcasts in other languages – in Spanish for Latin America and Spanish-speakers in the United States, for example.

MTV Europe is based in London, with regional offices around Europe. It reaches about 60 million homes in 37 countries 24 hours a day, has a 'Euro' style, and covers a wide range of topics of interest to young people, including fashion, sports, news and competitions. It is best known for its music shows and it runs the annual MTV Europe Music Awards. The company also takes seriously its responsibility to raise its audience's awareness of social issues; one MTV campaign was 'Vote Europe', to highlight the issues in European elections and to encourage young people to vote.

Ian Renwick is Vice President of Communications at MTV Europe. Thomas Madvig is a 'VJ' (video jockey), presenting news items to MTV viewers in English, his second language. Eva Hiltner has a customer service role, dealing in English and German with the cable operators who deliver MTV programmes to people's homes. Vanessa Sackarnd is a programming research analyst who analyses people's opinions of MTV and its programmes, assesses viewing figures for different markets, and investigates the habits and preferences of young people.

We would like to thank Ian Renwick, Thomas Madvig, Eva Hiltner, Vanessa Sackarnd, Jacquie Hewit and Polly Stevens for their help.

Intra

Intra is a Swedish market communications company with offices in Uppsala and Stockholm. Staff there plan, design, produce and distribute advertising and information campaigns for other businesses, using a range of traditional and interactive media. These might include print advertisements in newspapers and magazines; folders, brochures and catalogues; radio or television spots; events such as exhibitions; direct marketing, telemarketing, or Web sites. The company is particularly well-known for its work on behalf of high-profile Swedish businesses like the dairy company Arla and for information technology companies, and for its environmental concerns. Many of its clients are Swedish, but the company is increasingly developing its contacts in other countries and therefore beginning to do business in English.

Below the managing director of Intra, Leif Nordlund, are project managers, copy writers, art designers and Web and print specialists. Björn Falkenäs is the art director on some of Intra's projects and is also well-informed about green issues. Julia Edlund, a project manager, has been involved in work for the Finnish company Nokia, which meant using both English and Swedish, and she also communicates in English and French with an agency in Brussels that helps Intra find international contracts. Jacob Bergström is a graphic designer who works on concepts and design for print materials but is also proficient at working with interactive media like the Internet. His main use of English is on the Internet, where he looks for information and products as well as for well-designed sites.

We would like to thank Leif Nordlund, Björn Falkenäs, Julia Edlund, Jacob Bergström, Viktor Ahnfelt and Mia Ulim for their help

---

The aim of these two pages is to familiarise learners with the four companies that *More Work in Progress* focuses on. They also introduce them to some basic vocabulary and get learners to do a few of the tasks that are common in the Course Book.

First discuss what learners can see in the pictures on the two pages. Check that they know the names of the four companies. Find out if they know / can guess anything about them, e.g. what they do, nationality etc.

1 Demonstrate the task: ask *Which photo or text on page 5 is connected with W H Smith?* Elicit 2. In pairs, learners do the same for the other companies. Check answers.

2 Demonstrate the task: *Which company is this about?* Play the first extract. Elicit *Intra*. Play the other three extracts for learners to do the same. Learners check answers in pairs and as a class.

> 1 So we can design your Web site for you, but we suggest that you also run a television campaign. You can have a great Web site, but it's no good if no one knows it's there. So one reason for the TV ads would be to promote the Web site – to encourage people to visit it.
> 2 A: Can I pay in pounds for these?
>   B: Yes, certainly. Let me see. Er . . . the paper's 300 pesetas, those are five-fifty, so that's eight hundred and fifty pesetas, please.
> 3 Of course it's mainly a music channel, and the news we present is young people's news. It's about 50% music news and 50% social – anything that interests people between 15 and 25.
> 4 In this part of the factory everything is hand-made. Some of our most famous chocolates are produced here.

3 Demonstrate the task: *Which company is a manufacturer?* Elicit *Neuhaus*. If learners do not know *manufacturer*, encourage them to use their dictionaries before you confirm their ideas. In pairs, they match the companies with the other business areas. Check answers. Drill the business areas for correct pronunciation as necessary.

Key

1A W H Smith – 2   B Intra – 4
 C MTV – 3   D Neuhaus – 1
2 1 Intra 2 W H Smith 3 MTV 4 Neuhaus
3a Neuhaus b MTV c W H Smith d Intra

Departures

1A Background

Action

- **Describe places**
- **Ask for and give information**
- **Vocabulary: features of a location**
- **Grammar: question forms**

Introduction

Each learner thinks of three towns or cities, anywhere in the world: one they like, one they dislike, and one they would like to visit, and the reasons for their choices. They discuss their choices in small groups and as a class.

Speaking and Reading: describing places

1 a Copy the chart onto the board. Demonstrate the task: ask *What other words can we use to describe geography?* Write their answers on the board. In pairs, learners do the same with the other headings. Write their ideas on the board. Next refer them to the word list on page 11. Compare the words under people, business activities and geography with the list on the board. Check learners understand *coast* and *temperature* /ˈtemprətʃə/ for the next exercise. Drill the vocabulary for correct pronunciation as necessary.
b and c In pairs, learners use the words and phrases on the board to discuss their towns. Make sure they make notes for Exercise 6. Two pairs compare ideas and then discuss as a class.

2 a Find out what learners know about Alicante (e.g. location, climate, main industries, size). Elicit what they can see in the photographs.
b Learners match the photographs with the texts. Check answers in pairs and as a class.
c Learners read the first text again and discuss the question in pairs. Get quick feedback. Correct any pronunciation errors with the vocabulary from Exercise 1.

Key

2a 1 Alicante airport   2 Isabel and Andrew   3 Alicante
2b A3,   B1,   C2

Speaking and Writing: asking for information

3 Refer learners to the first answer. Ask *What's the question?* Elicit *Where's Alicante?* and write it on the board. In pairs, learners make questions for the other answers. Elicit their answers and write them on the board. Leave part of the board free for the chart in Exercise 4. Discuss when we use the question words, e.g. *when* for time, *how many* for quantity, etc. Drill the questions and answers for correct stress and intonation. In pairs, learners take it in turns to ask and answer. Leave the questions on the board for the next exercise.

Key

3 • Where's Alicante?
- What's the population? / How many people live in Alicante?
- Why do tourists come to Alicante?
- How many sunny days are there each year?
- What's the average temperature?
- How many people use the airport each year?
- Who uses the airport?
- Who are Isabel and Andrew?
- Where is Isabel from? / Where does Isabel come from?
- Where were they in the early 1990s?
- When did they open the shop in Alicante?

Grammar: question forms

4 a Copy the table onto the board. Elicit the verb form in the first question in Exercise 3. Learners do the same with the other questions. Complete the table on the board as a class.
b Write the two questions on the board. Ask *What is the subject of the question?* Elicit *How many people*. Then ask *What's the answer?* Establish that questions and answers that have the same subject do not need an auxiliary verb. Follow the same procedure with the second question and establish that *where* is not the subject of the question, and that an auxiliary verb is needed. Use the board to highlight their answers as below:

How many people live in Alicante?

↓

260,000 (subject)

Where does Isabel come from?

↘

She comes from Barcelona. (object)

c Refer learners to the first answer. Ask *What's the question?* Elicit *Is Alicante in Portugal?* and write it on the board. In pairs, learners make questions for the other answers. Write their answers on the board and drill for correct pronunciation.

5 In pairs, learners write 10 questions they want to ask Isabel and Andrew. Make sure they keep them for Unit 4. Alternatively write *Isabel*, *Andrew* and *W H Smith* on three large separate pieces of paper. Divide learners into small groups. Give each group one piece of paper. Allow learners enough time to write three or four questions as a group. Then rotate the pieces of paper. Follow the same procedure until each group has written questions for each subject. For feedback, read out all the questions, or get a representative from each group to do so. Correct any errors as a class. Keep the questions for Unit 4.

Key

4a

When	did	they open the shop in Alicante?
How many people	live	in Alicante?
	use	the airport each year?
Why	do	tourists come to Alicante?
Who	uses	the airport?
	are	Isabel and Andrew?
Where	is	Alicante?
	is	Isabel from?
	does	Isabel come from?
	were	they in the early 1990s?
What	is	the population?
	is	the average temperature?

b There is no auxiliary verb *do* in the first question because *how many people* is the subject of the question. In the second question, there is the auxiliary verb *does* because *Isabel* is the subject of the question, not *where*.

c • Has Alicante got good facilities / a wonderful climate / beautiful beaches / an airport?
  • Do Isabel and Andrew work for W H Smith?
  • Is Isabel Spanish? / Is Isabel from Barcelona?
  • Was Andrew in Britain in 1995?
  • Did the shop open in 1995?

Extra practice

Play *Who am I?* Check learners know *alive* and *dead*. Divide learners into teams. First demonstrate the activity: think of a famous person or someone the learners know, e.g. a colleague. Explain they have to guess who the person is. They can ask 10 questions (*yes / no* or *wh-* questions) but you will only answer if the questions are grammatically correct. The teams take it in turns to ask the questions. The first team to guess within 10 questions wins. Next, each team thinks of two people. They play the game in the same way.

Talking point

See note on page 5.

Writing: giving information

6 Refer learners back to their notes from Exercise 1 and the first text in Exercise 2. In pairs, they write a short description of their town for a tourist brochure. Pairs exchange texts. They correct any errors they find, note down any ideas that they like and give them back. They then write a final text with corrections and any new ideas from the other text they have read. If you wish, display the descriptions for the other learners to read. If possible, find a text from a real tourist brochure for them to compare with their own text.

1B W H Smith

Action

- **Give and ask about reasons**
- **Listen to reasons**
- **Vocabulary: compound nouns, airport shops and purchases**

Speaking: airport shops and purchases

1 Draw a mindmap on the board:

Ask *What do people want to buy at airports?* Elicit one or two items and write them on the board. In pairs, learners do the same. Use the board to collate their ideas. Make sure they keep this list for Exercise 7. Next indicate an item on the board and ask *What kind of shop do they need?* Write their answer next to the item. Do the same for the other items in pairs or as a class. Drill for correct pronunciation.

2 Direct learners to the photograph. Elicit what they can see on the shelves. List new vocabulary on the board. Discuss other things W H Smith sells.

Extra practice

Write these questions on the board. Learners discuss the questions in small groups.
- **Which airports have you flown from?**
- **What did you buy?**
- **What did you think of the shops?**
- **What would you like to be able to buy at an airport?**

Reading: background information

Write these questions on the board:
- **What do you think W H Smith sells?**
- **How many shops do you think it has?**
- **How many people do you think it employs in total?**
- **Is there a similar chain of shops in your country? What's its name?**

Learners discuss their ideas. Then they read the text to see if their ideas were correct. Check learners understand *chain of shops*.

3 If you wish, write the verbs on the board:

employ   move   own   be   open

Learners read the first sentence. Elicit the verb and tense. Learners complete the text. Check answers. Discuss **b** as a class.

Key

3a 1 opened 2 was 3 were 4 moved
      5 are 6 owns 7 employs

b Because travellers want to buy what they sell for their journey, e.g. newspapers, sweets..

Vocabulary: compound nouns

4 a Refer learners back to the text in Exercise 3. Demonstrate the task: ask *What do you call bookshops in railway stations?* Write **station bookshops** on the board. Learners find the other compound nouns. Compare answers in pairs and as a class.

b Divide learners into pairs. Ask one pair to read out the example exchange. Learners take it in turns to ask and answer in the same way. To check answers, volunteer pairs roleplay their exchanges.

c Copy the exercise onto the board. In small groups, learners brainstorm as many compound nouns as they can. If you wish, give them a time limit. Write their ideas on the board.

Key

4a • station bookshops • high street shops • airport shops • computer games • city centres

b • street market: It's a market in a street.
• traveller's cheque: It's a cheque for a traveller.
• address book: It's a book where you write addresses.
• cash machine: It's a machine where you can get cash.
• newspaper stand: It's where you can buy a newspaper.
• telephone card: It's a card that you can use to pay for a phone call.

c • telephone + box, card, book / directory, number, call
• cash, membership, name / business, cheque / bank, charge, post, birthday, credit, telephone, playing + card

---

Listening and Speaking: giving reasons

5 Refer learners to the three questions. Discuss them as a class. Play the tape. Compare learners' ideas with what Carmen says.

A lot of our customers are British, of course – especially on Tuesdays and Saturdays when the charter flights come in. But we speak English in the shop with everyone except Spanish people. They come in to buy a newspaper or a magazine for the plane. Some people are impatient or rude because they're in a hurry. Other people have a lot of time before they catch their plane, so they stop and chat. We can do that on quiet days – but on Saturdays there are long queues. Then some people come for help – they can't find a cash machine, or they want to know where Burger King is. They have all kinds of problems.

6 a Copy the four sentences onto the board. Play the tape again, stopping after *'for the plane'*. Complete the first sentence on the board. Play the rest of the tape. Learners compare answers in pairs. Complete the sentences on the board. Then direct learners to the Phrasebook. Indicate the first sentence on the board and ask *Which sentence has the same construction?* Elicit *To pass the time*. Write it on the board under the first sentence. Highlight the infinitive form. Do the same with the other sentences, highlighting the different constructions to give reasons.

b Demonstrate the task: indicate the first sentence on the board and say *What question can you ask?* Elicit *Why do they come in?* Learners write questions for the other sentences. Compare answers in pairs and as a class.

c In pairs, learners complete the sentences to mean the same as the ones in **a**. If you wish, write their answers on the board under the original sentences.

7 Demonstrate the task: ask *Why do people buy a newspaper when they arrive at an airport?* Elicit their ideas, making sure they use the language from Exercise 6. Now ask *Why do people buy a newspaper when they leave an airport?* Get the learners to read out the reasons in the Phrasebook. Divide learners into pairs. Refer them back to their list of purchases in Exercise 1. **A**s ask about when people arrive at an airport and **B**s ask about when people leave an airport. Monitor and note down any errors you hear with the expressions for giving reasons. Compare ideas and finally use the board to correct any errors.

8 Learners read the instructions. Check they understand *mail order catalogues*. Divide them into pairs. Explain that they must decide on one product, who is going to buy it, and where they are going to sell it and why. Monitor and help. Learners tell the class what they have decided. In a large class, they can report back in groups.

Key

5a Carmen doesn't mention this. Perhaps because it is a very busy airport and a lot of the customers are British and so they already know W H Smith.

b To buy a newspaper or magazine or to ask for help.

c They need to speak English, be polite, patient, efficient, able to work under pressure. They need to know about the airport.

6a • to buy • because • so • for

b • Why do they come into the shop?
• Why are some people impatient or rude?
• Why do some people stop and chat?
Why do other people come into the shop?

c • ... they want to buy a newspaper or a magazine.
• ... they are impatient or rude.
• ... a chat, because they have a lot of time before they catch their plane.
• ... they need some help.

1C Taking off

Action

- **Understand signs**
- **Understand and give directions**
- **Listen for directions**
- **Vocabulary: airport facilities and airport procedures**
- **Grammar: modal verbs**

Speaking: understanding signs

In pairs or as a class, learners brainstorm the things that they expect to find in an airport. Compare their ideas with the signs and list in Exercise 1.

1 Learners look at the list of facilities and signs and discuss the three questions. Check as a class. Establish the difference between *ground floor* and *first floor*. Drill for correct pronunciation as necessary.

Key

1a A bar   B coffee shop   C car hire   D chemist's
E airport information   F meeting point   G arrivals
H departures   I escalator   J stairs

b meeting point (F), escalator (I), stairs (J)

c • the departure area: second floor
• the arrivals hall: ground floor
• W H Smith: second floor
• the car hire office: ground floor

Extra practice

P 1.1 To practise the compound nouns in this unit,
photocopy the worksheet on page 76 for each group. Cut the
words up as indicated. Learners work in groups of four. Each
group lays the words face down on the table. The first student
turns over two cards, e.g. *newspaper*, *lounge*. If the words can
form a compound noun, they keep the pair and have another
turn. If the words do not match, they turn them over and leave
them in the same position. The next learner does the same.
The aim is to collect as many compound nouns as possible.

Listening: directions

2 a Books closed. Write these questions on the board:

What do they want?   Where do they need to go?

Play the tape. Compare answers in pairs and as a class.
Books open. Learners listen to the conversations again and
write in the missing words. Check answers in pairs. Write
their answers on the board. If you wish, play the tape again
for learners to shadow the conversations.

 (T = traveller   R = Raquel)

T: *Can you help me, please? I must change my pesetas back
into pounds before I leave.*

R: *Yes, well the exchange bureau is on this floor, but it's over
there in the departure lounge. I'm afraid you can't change
money until you go through the security check.*

T: *Oh, right. Thank you.*

(T = traveller   N = Nuria)

T: *Excuse me. I left my bag here somewhere and now I can't
find it.*

N: *You needn't worry. The security guards have probably
taken it. You should ask at the Lost and Found office. It's
downstairs, on the ground floor. You can use the stairs,
just there, or the escalators.*

T: *Oh, thanks a lot.*

Key

2a The first person wants to change some pesetas into
pounds. He needs to go to the exchange bureau in the
departure lounge.
The second person wants to find her bag. She needs to
go to the Lost and Found office on the ground floor.

b See tapescript.

Grammar: modal verbs

3 a Demonstrate the task: say *Find the first verb that is
followed by another verb*. Elicit *Can you help me?* and write
it on the board. Learners find the other examples in the
conversations. Write them on the board. Discuss the
question. Highlight the infinitives on the board.

b–d Learners discuss the exercise in pairs and as a class.
Finally, refer learners back to the sentences on the board.
Use these questions to check understanding: *Which one
means not necessary / not possible / not able / a good idea /
possible / necessary?*

Key

3a Infinitive without *to*.

b • obligation: You must change …
• advice: You should change …
• possibility: You can change …

c • ability   • permission

d You shouldn't leave your luggage here = It is not a good
idea.
You mustn't leave your luggage here = It is not
permitted.
You can't leave your luggage here = It is not permitted.
You needn't leave your luggage here = It is not necessary.

Vocabulary: airport procedures

4 Refer learners to the procedures in the exercise. Ask *Which
one should your friend do first?* Reach an agreement as a
class. Then in small groups they discuss the order. If you
wish, discuss their ideas as a class and agree the best
procedure. Then copy these onto the board:

**can('t)   should(n't)
must(n't)   need(n't)**

Learners work in pairs. Explain that they must roleplay what
they would say to their friend. Read out the example together
as a class. Establish that they must use the modal verbs on
the board as often as possible. Monitor and correct any
errors you hear.

Key

4   suggested answer
arrive early; check in; get your boarding card; go through
security checks; have a drink; watch the departures
board; wait in the departure lounge; phone me; board the
plane

Extra practice

Write these sentence beginnings on the board:

I must ....

I can't ....

I needn't ....

My boss / teacher should ....

My colleagues / classmates shouldn't ....

My best friend can ....

I mustn't ....

Each learner completes the sentences about themselves. Four
sentences must be true and three must be false, e.g. *I should*

give up smoking (False because I don't smoke). Learners work in small groups. One learner reads out their first sentence. The others can ask five questions to see if the sentence is true or false, e.g. *What kind of cigarettes do you smoke? How many do you smoke a day?* etc. Then they say if it's true or false. If they guess incorrectly, the learner gets a point.

Speaking: directions

5 Divide learners into pairs: **As** are the shop assistants and **Bs** are the customers. Check they understand the information about their roles. They roleplay their conversations. Monitor and note down any errors you hear. Then they change roles. Follow the same procedure. Finally, use the board to correct any errors when the task is finished.

Grammar backup 1

Question forms

Key

1b Who   **c** What   **d** Why   **e** How many   **f** Where
 g When
2b Where did you go yesterday?
 c When are they going on holiday?
 d Where did you meet Tom?
 e Who faxed the report?
 f How many languages can you speak?
 g Why are you learning English?
3b When **is he** going to write to them?
 c How many meetings has **she got** next week?
 d **What** is your name?
 e Yes, I **do**.
 f **Have** you got / **Do** you have much work to do today?
 g Yes, I **will**.

Modal verbs

Key

1b should   **c** can't   **d** can   **e** can't / mustn't
 f needn't   **g** must   **h** shouldn't
2b He **must go** to Germany tomorrow for a meeting.
 c He **mustn't** tell her. It's a secret.
 d **Can** he speak Spanish fluently?
 e When **should we** leave this evening?

Purchases

2A On the till

Action

- Listen to a shop transaction
- Deal with foreign currency transactions
- Grammar: question tags

Speaking and Listening: a shop transaction

Brainstorm what learners expect to find in a W H Smith shop and write their ideas on the board.

1 Learners look at the objects in the pictures. Compare them with the ones on the board. Learners discuss **b** and **c** in pairs and as a class. Do not confirm their answers yet.

2 Play the tape for learners to answer the questions. Check answers. Compare them with their ideas from Exercise 1.

(C = customer   N = Nuria)
C: I'd like this magazine, please.
N: Right. Are you paying in pounds?
C: No, pesetas. This one's six hundred pesetas, isn't it?
N: Let's see … yes, that's right.
C: Here you are. A thousand.
N: Thanks. Here's your change.
C: Thank you.
N: Would you like a bag?
C: Yes, please. Thanks.
N: I've seen you before, haven't I? Do you live here?
C: Yes, we moved here last year.
N: Oh, right. See you again, then.
C: Yeah, bye.

3 Learners read the exercise. Play the first line. Elicit which expression the boy uses. Then play the whole conversation for learners to do the same. Check answers.

Key

1b • The shop accepts credit cards.
• He's paying in cash (pesetas).
• He probably isn't Spanish because he moved to Alicante last year and has an English accent.
• He's interested in motorbikes.
• They're kept on the wall behind the assistant / till.
c D, C, B, E, A
2b one thousand pesetas   c four hundred pesetas
3 See tapescript.

Grammar: question tags

4 **a** Copy the two questions in the exercise onto the board. Ask *Does the speaker's voice rise or fall at the end of the question?* Play the tape. Mark the intonation on the board and discuss why the patterns are different. Follow the same procedure for **b**.
c Discuss as a class and highlight the form on the board.
d Discuss in pairs and as a class. Highlight the form on the board. Finally, discuss if learners have question tags in their own languages and how they form / use them.

How much is it?
Are you paying in pounds?
This one's 600 pesetas, isn't it? (x2)

5 **a** Learners do the exercise. Check answers. Then in pairs, **A** says the questions and **B** says if **A** is checking information or is unsure. Make sure they change roles.
b Demonstrate the task: learners write down six things they think they know about you. Then they check the things on their list by asking you tag questions. Only answer if the questions are grammatically correct and the intonation is appropriate. Learners then do the same in pairs.

Key

4a *How much is it?* It falls because it is a *wh-* question.
Are you paying in pounds? It rises because it is a *yes / no* question.
b 1 The speaker's voice falls because he is checking information that he is fairly sure of.
2 The speaker's voice rises because he is unsure.
c The question is formed with a sentence and a tag. The verb in the sentence is positive. The verb in the tag is negative and comes before the subject, *it*. The subject in the sentence, *this*, is replaced by the subject, *it*, in the tag.
d See Grammar backup 2.
5a • You're Andrew, aren't you?
• A plane has just arrived from Britain, hasn't it?
• We've got some new magazines, haven't we?
• I can go now, can't I?
• She enjoys her work, doesn't she?
• We took more money yesterday, didn't we?

Extra practice

P 2.1   Photocopy the worksheet on page 76 for each learner. In pairs, they complete the sentences with names of other learners in the class. Then they mingle and ask tag questions to check the information using the appropriate intonation. They report back their findings to the class.

Listening and Speaking: foreign currency transactions

6 Learners read the conversation and predict what Nuria and the customer say. Play the tape to check their answers.

(N = Nuria   C = customer)
N: Hello. Can I help you?
C: Yes, I'd like this book, please, but I've only got pounds.
N: That's all right. We take pounds. What does the price tag say?
C: Er … one thousand one hundred pesetas.
C: One thousand one hundred. That's five pounds, please.

7 Learners roleplay the conversation in pairs. Make sure they change roles. Correct any errors on the board at the end.

Key

6 See tapescript.
7a 220   b film £3.50; guidebook £9.00; paperback £6.00; chocolate £1.00

2B On display

Action

- Find out about layouts and displays
- Listen to an interview
- Make and respond to suggestions
- Vocabulary: locations, referring words

Speaking and Reading: shop layouts

1 Write the names of some shops on the board that you and the learners are familiar with. Discuss **a** and find out which shop layouts they like / dislike and why. Then discuss **b**.

2 Write 1–13 on the board. Learners read the description and label where the products are on the plan. Check answers in pairs. Write the items on the board. Check answers from Exercise 1.

Key

2 A9 B11 C8 D13 E1 / 2 F10 G1 / 2 H7 I6 J5 K4

Talking point

See note on page 5.

Vocabulary: locations and referring words

3 Copy the exercise onto the board. Do the first one together and write the answer on the board. Learners do the exercise. Write their answers on the board.

4 Demonstrate the task: read the first two lines and ask *Who is 'you'?* Learners do the exercise. Compare answers in pairs and as a class.

Key

3a near **b** far **c** back **d** left-hand **e** front **f** closer to
4a the customer **b** after you have picked up a paper
  c in front of the shop **d** the central display unit
  e the right-hand counter **f** the shelves on the left-hand
    side **g** the wall on the right

Extra practice

P 2.2 Photocopy the worksheet on page 77. Learners work in pairs. Each learner has a plan of the shop and its contents and one blank layout. Establish that they are standing at the front of the shop. **A** describes their plan to **B** who draws it. **B** then describes their plan for **A** to draw. When they have finished, they compare plans to check answers.

Listening to an interview

5 Learners discuss the questions in pairs. Compare ideas as a class. Play the tape to see if their ideas were correct.

 In the summer we have English books and English magazines next to each other. As you walk in through the main door you'll see English books and magazines, for the simple reason that the majority of our customers in that period are English. Now in November, probably next week, we'll be looking to move it around so that the Spanish books and Spanish magazines are the ones that you see as soon as you go in the door, because the majority of the customers that you get between now and May next year are Spanish nationals. It's very seasonal.

We have the sweets right in front of the window, for the simple reason that you see it and it attracts the attention. It's bright, it's lit up, you've got all the Mars products on top so the children see it. If the parents get dragged in, the kid's going to have a sweet and the mum and dad might buy a magazine.

And we obviously put all the children's books etc. together, so we've got a Disney section which is right next to the children's books. The Disney section's bright and colourful, and it's got things from Pocahontas, from the Hunchback of Notre Dame, Toy Story, as well as Mickey Mouse, so nine times out of ten a young child will walk in through the door, see that, and they're immediately brought over there. Once they're over there, there's the books as well.

Behind the till we've got tobacco because it's more often than not an impulse purchase. We've got a chewing gum display unit next to the till, which we sell a lot, for the simple reason that people pick up a newspaper and as they're paying for it they'll just pick up a packet of chewing gum. And then behind the till as well we've got things like batteries and films, because if anyone's going to take anything out of our shop batteries and films are quite high-risk areas.

Key

5a The display changes in November and May. In summer they have English books and magazines facing the main door because most customers are British. In winter most customers are Spanish, so the Spanish books and magazines face the door.

b The sweets are in front of the window and are brightly lit so that children can see them easily. If parents buy them sweets, they may also buy a magazine at the same time.

c The children's books are next to the Disney display which is bright and colourful and will attract them.

d An 'impulse purchase' is something you suddenly decide to buy although you did not plan to buy it before you went in.

e The chewing gum is next to the till, so that people pick up a packet when they are buying something else.

f Batteries and films. High-risk items are things that people may steal, so they are kept behind the till where it is difficult for customers to take them.

Listening and Speaking: making suggestions

6 Learners discuss the exercise in pairs or as a class.

7 Check learners understand *stuff, freezer* and *frozen*. Learners listen to the conversation and answer the questions. Check answers.

A: *The trouble is that people are only buying the fresh meat. We're not selling anything at all from the freezer.*

B: *Shall we stop selling the frozen stuff, then?*

A: *No, I don't think that's the answer. Some people want frozen meat, so we need to have it there. I suppose we could move the freezer.*

B: *Yes, or replace it with one with a clear top, so customers can see what's in it.*

A: *Hey, that's a good idea. Right, let's buy a new freezer. And why don't we put up some signs to draw attention to the frozen meat?*

B: *Good idea. Oh, and have you thought about doing some special offers? Two for the price of one. Just for a week or so. It might help.*

A: *OK. Let's try.*

8 Copy the exercise onto the board. Play the conversation again for learners to complete the expressions. Write their answers on the board. Elicit the form of the verbs and highlight them on the board. If you wish, copy this chart onto the board:

agree	disagree

Play the conversation again for learners to note down the expressions that the speakers use to agree and disagree with suggestions. Write their answers on the board. Finally, direct learners to the Phrasebook. Elicit which expressions are missing from the list on the board. Write them in the chart and highlight the verb forms. Drill the expressions for correct stress and intonation.

9 Explain that the teaching room is going to become a branch of W H Smith. First, in pairs, learners list the items that they are going to stock. Then they discuss the layout and draw a plan. If you wish, they can show their plans to the class to decide which one is best.

Key

6 They are discussing the display. They are probably talking about ways of changing it.

7 a It's a butcher's shop / supermarket.
b No one is buying the frozen meat.
c To move the freezer, buy a freezer with a clear top, put up signs or special offers on frozen meat.
8 See tapescript.
a–d are followed by the infinitive without *to*. **e** is followed by *-ing*.

Extra practice

Copy the expressions for giving suggestions onto cards and distribute them amongst the learners. Each learner thinks of a problem; it can be real or imaginary. Learners then mingle and ask for suggestions using the expressions on their cards. At the end of each exchange, they swap their cards so they practise using different expressions.

2C On holiday

Action

- **Read and write a postcard**
- **Describe holiday gifts**
- **Listen to a conversation**
- **Express likes and preferences**
- **Grammar: numbers and quantities**

Introduction

Discuss learners' last holiday; where, when, why they went and what they did. Find out if they wrote any postcards and, if so, who they sent them to and what kinds of things they wrote about.

Reading: a holiday postcard

1 a Learners read the postcard and answer the questions. Check as a class. See if the postcard is similar to ones they write on holiday.
b Learners read the sentences. Demonstrate the task: ask *Where can the first sentence go in the postcard?* Elicit the answer. Learners do the same with the other sentences. Compare answers in pairs. Then volunteers read out their postcards, stopping after one of the extra sentences; the other learners decide if they think it is in the best position.
c Discuss as a class. Find out if learners use the same features when writing a postcard in their own language.

Key

1a • daily life on holiday – paragraph 2
• Sue's general opinion of the holiday – paragraph 1
• a future plan – paragraph 1
b • ... some shopping. **It's not very far on the train.**
• ... the beach. **It's crowded but beautiful, and the sea is warm.**
• ... too hard! **I'm looking forward to seeing you all.**
• ... the office. **What a change from Birmingham!**
• ... some shopping. **I want to buy some presents before we leave. It's not very far on the train.**
c The beginning (Dear Everyone) and ending (Love); short forms (it's etc.); adjectives like 'great' and 'fantastic'; phrases like 'really hot'; the use of exclamation marks.

Speaking: holiday gifts

2 a Direct learners to the picture. Find out if they know what it is or if they like it. Discuss the exercise in small groups or as a class.
b Explain that learners are going to open a gift shop in a holiday town in their country. First they make a list of ten items that they will stock. Then they discuss their ideas in small groups and decide on a final list. They report their decision to the class.

Listening to a conversation

3 Copy this onto the board:

positive	negative

To check understanding, learners categorise the adjectives in **b**. Write their answers on the board. Drill for correct pronunciation as necessary. Next play the tape for learners to answer **a** and **b**. Check answers. In pairs, learners think of other adjectives. Write their ideas on the board. Leave them there for Exercise 5.

 (D = Dave   S = Sue)

D: *Oh, I'll buy some wine for Kevin. It's cheaper than in England. Look at those pots. Would Jane like one of those? Or a basket?*

S: *I don't think she'd like either of them much. Anyway they're difficult to carry home. Maybe a pair of these sandals.*

D: *Oh, yes, they're quite nice. In fact I think she'd love them. Now Tom ...*

S: *He'd be happy with a stuffed donkey, or a doll. That's fun, or one of those mugs. Which shall we get?*

D: *None of them. They're all awful. Completely tasteless.*

S: *So? He's only nine. Let's get him the doll. Now, who else? Your mother ...*

D: *She doesn't really need any of these things. Well, perhaps the tablecloth?*

S: *Yes, it's lovely. Or would she prefer something to eat – this ... um ... turrón?*

D: *No, look, it's got nuts in it. The tablecloth, then. Right, so what have we decided?*

Key

3a They will probably buy wine, sandals, a doll and a tablecloth.

b cheap – wine; fun – doll; quite nice – sandals; tasteless / awful – stuffed donkey, doll, mug; lovely – tablecloth

Grammar: numbers and quantities

4 a Direct learners to the sentences in the exercise. Ask *What are they talking about in each sentence?* Play the tape. Stop after each sentence and check answers as a class.

b Copy this onto the board:

choice of two things	choice of more than two things

Demonstrate the task: ask *How many things does 'either of them' refer to?* Elicit *two* and write **either of them** in the first column. Learners categorise the other expressions in the same way. Check in pairs and write their answers on the board.

c and d Learners discuss the questions in pairs and as a class.

Key

4a a pot; a pot or a basket; a stuffed donkey, a doll or a mug; the things in the shop

b choice of two things: either of them, one of them, neither of them, both of them
choice of more than two things: one of them, none of them, (not) any of them, all of them, some of them

c • not one, not any = none   • not either = neither

d • *We don't want none of those postcards.* Incorrect (double negative).
• *I like both of these dolls; I'd be happy with either of them.* Correct.
• *Neither of them isn't very attractive.* Incorrect (double negative).

Speaking: likes and preferences

Copy the Phrasebook onto the board. Highlight the verb forms.

5 Direct learners to the pictures. In pairs, they decide which gifts they would like to receive and why. Compare ideas as a class.

Writing a postcard

6 Learners write a similar postcard to the one in Exercise 1 from a holiday town, but they must not mention its name. They read out their postcard for the others to guess where it is. Use the board to correct any errors at the end of the exercise. Finally decide as a class which holiday sounds the best.

Grammar backup 2

Question tags

Key

1b aren't I?   **c** has it?   **d** can't she?
e were there?   **f** have they?   **g** don't they?
h have I?   **i** doesn't he?   **j** didn't you?

2b **He needs** to arrive early, doesn't he?
c She's never rude, **is** she?
d There are two faxes on your desk, aren't **there**?
e She doesn't have to wear a uniform, **does** she?
f We can't see the manager, **can** we?

Numbers and quantities

Key

1b most   **c** Either   **d** One   **e** None   **f** any
2b all   **c** any   **d** some   **e** None   **f** One
g both   **h** Neither

3A Careers

> ### Action
>
> - Read and write about careers
> - Vocabulary: *work for / work as*
> - Grammar: past continuous

Introduction

Bring in photographs of two friends or members of your family. Get learners to ask questions about their jobs, e.g. *What does he do? Has he always had the same job? Which job did he like the most / least? Why? What job would he like to have?* Then learners interview each other about their own careers and the careers of members of their family. Encourage them to make notes on what their partner says about one person for Exercise 5.

Reading about careers

1 Learners look at the photographs of Andrew and Isabel. Elicit what they remember about them from Unit 1. Then learners read the texts and complete the career histories. Check answers.

> **Key**
>
> | 1 | Isabel | **1992–1995** Manager . . . |
> |---|---|---|
> | | | **1991–1992** Deputy manager . . . |
> | | | **1990–1991** Sales assistant . . . |
> | | Andrew | **1995–now** Deputy manager . . . |
> | | | **1994–1995** W H Smith management training . . . |
> | | | **1990–1994** Sales assistant . . . |

Vocabulary: *work for / work as*

2 Learners look at the text about Isabel again and answer **a** and **b**. Check answers. To check that learners understand that *work for* is followed by the name of the company / employer and that *to work as* is followed by the name of a job, copy **to work for +** and **to work as +** onto the board. Complete as a class. Then learners do **c** in pairs or as a class.

> **Key**
>
> **2a** She worked for Paperchase. She worked as a sales assistant.
>
> **b** She worked for Paperchase. She worked as (a) deputy manager.

Grammar: past continuous

Copy this onto the board:

- **Isabel .... (work) as a sales assistant .... before she .... (become) the manager of the Victoria branch.**
- **While she .... (run) the shop, she also .... (attend) training courses.**

Learners fill in the missing verbs and then check their answers with Isabel's career history. Complete the sentences on the board.

3 Learners discuss the exercise in pairs or as a class. Use the sentences on the board to highlight their answers. To check concept, draw these two timelines on the board:

Elicit which timeline illustrates which sentence.

4 **a** Learners discuss what is happening in the pictures. Supply unknown vocabulary as necessary, e.g. *to force something open, to turn the electricity on, fuse box.*
b Elicit an example sentence. In pairs, learners write sentences in the same way. To check answers, learners read out their sentences.

> **Key**
>
> **3a** The second sentence. 'Running the shop' covered the whole period. She attended training courses at different times during that period of time.
>
> **b** It tells us that one activity (working as a sales assistant) finished before the other (being deputy manager) began. The past simple tense is used.
>
> **c** While he was studying, he also worked part-time . . .
>
> **d** While I was studying, I also worked part-time . . .
> Past simple verb forms do not change. Past continuous auxiliary verb forms change: I / she / he / it + was; you / we / they + were.
>
> **4b suggested answers**
> While the customers were trying to get in, an assistant was trying to force the till open. While the assistants were stopping customers from getting in, another assistant was receiving a delivery. While the assistants were cleaning the display cases, another one was putting up a poster.
> When the new manager arrived, the assistants were working in the dark / an assistant was trying to turn the electricity back on / one assistant was having a drink / the deputy manager was giving orders.

Extra practice

P 3.1 Learners work in small groups. Photocopy a worksheet on page 77 for each group. Divide the cut-up story amongst the learners in each group. Explain that together the slips make one story which they have to put in the correct order. They cannot look at each others' slips. The learner who thinks they have the beginning of the story reads it out. The next learner does the same. As they agree a possible order, they put their slip face down on the table until the whole story has been sequenced. Alternatively, they can stand in a line in the order they have agreed. To check answers, each group reads out their first slips to the whole class. Together decide which order is best until the whole story is revealed. Then in their groups, learners fill in the gaps with the past simple or past continuous.

Writing a career history

5 Learners make notes and then write a career history. Alternatively, if they did the activity in the introduction, learners ask their partner questions to check that their notes are accurate. Then they write about their partner or a member of their partner's family. If you did not use the warm-up, learners can make notes about themselves. They give their notes to their partner who uses them to write a career history. Finally, learners read each others' texts and check for grammatical and factual errors. If you wish, discuss which career history looks the most interesting.

3B Paperwork

Action

- **Read correspondence**
- **Open formal and informal letters**
- **Write a reply to a fax**
- **Vocabulary: verbs for placing orders**

Reading correspondence

1 **a** In pairs, give learners two minutes to list different kinds of correspondence. Write their ideas on the board. Then they look at the ones in the book to see if they are included in their list.
b and c Learners read the correspondence again and answer the questions. Check answers.

Key

1a • faxes – A, B   • invoice – C   • despatch note – D
b • A   • C   • B,D
c a request for payment – C
a list that arrives with a delivery – D
a request for a catalogue – A   for information only – B

Vocabulary: verbs for placing orders

2 Demonstrate the task: get learners to find *sourcing* in A. Ask *What will the school do after they see the catalogue?* Elicit their answers and then discuss the meaning of *source*. Learners do the same for the other verbs. Check answers in pairs and as a class.

3 Learners complete the sentences. Check answers.

4 **a** Write **Further to ...** on the board. Learners find the phrase in the faxes. Highlight the language which follows on the board.
b Copy this onto the board:

more formal ◄—————————► **less formal**

First learners find the two phrases that end the faxes. Write them in the appropriate place on the line. In pairs, they categorise the other endings. Check as a class. Refer learners to the Phrasebook. Discuss how they would end faxes, letters and messages in their own language.

Key

2A *source:* they will buy / order some books.
forward: she should send it to Andrew.
B *confirm:* Yes, she did.
book: She will phone a hotel.
C *recommend:* they should sell for £5.99
D *despatch:* they came from W H Smith (Branch 7985).
pack: they were put into boxes.
order: Andrew or Isabel (W H Smith Alicante) asked for them.
deliver: they are in Spain.
3a booked   **b** confirm   **c** recommend   **d** delivered
e order
4a our conversation / my fax
4b **more formal:** Yours faithfully; Yours sincerely; Yours; Regards; With best wishes; Many thanks; All the best; See you soon; **less formal:** Love

Extra practice

This activity revises verbs from Exercise 3. Learners work in small teams. Read out each definition below. The first team to say the right verb, gets a point.

1 to suggest something is a good idea. (to recommend)
2 to send something. (to despatch)
3 to send a message on to someone else. (to forward)
4 to find out where you get something from. (to source)
5 to say that something planned is definite. (to confirm)
6 to reserve a table in a restaurant. (to book)
7 to take / transport something to a country / building. (to deliver)
8 to put something in a box. (to pack)
9 to ask for something from a company. You may have to wait for it! (to order)

Writing: a reply to a fax

5 Copy this onto the board:
Who is writing?
Who are they writing to?
What do they want to say?
In pairs, learners choose fax A or D. They discuss the questions and make notes. Remind them of the expressions in the Phrasebook. Then they write their reply. They swap their replies with another pair who answered the same fax. They check for detail and correct any errors.

3C Sales skills

Action

- Listen to interviews
- Talk about skills and qualities
- Read about work experience
- Give an interview
- Grammar: *used to*

Speaking and Listening: skills and qualities

1 **a** Find out if any of the learners have worked as a sales assistant. Discuss the qualities that a sales assistant needs. Write learners' ideas on the board. Play the tape for them to see if their ideas are the same. Check answers in pairs and on the board.

b Learners discuss the exercise.

 It is very important for sales staff to speak at least some English. The shop is in an international airport, and W H Smith is a British company, so customers expect it. If staff can say hello, talk about prices and give directions in English … that's the minimum I need from them. Most of them speak much better English than that, though.
When I choose new staff, I also look at their experience, but they haven't all worked in shops before and of course we train them. They have to handle money and people confidently. Personality is very important. Staff must be warm and open with customers and very patient and polite, even when people are being difficult. In quiet periods some customers want a chat while they wait for their plane, and that's fine. Some need help, so staff give a lot of information and advice which is not really part of the job.
They are normally expected to wear a red W H Smith T-shirt, so customers can identify them – that's the uniform. We're open seven days a week, from seven in the morning to ten at night – and to midnight sometimes in the summer if there are a lot of night flights – so we all work different hours, and the shifts are quite complicated. People need to be flexible. In fact we're only closed on three days a year, when there are no newspaper deliveries.

Key

1a She wants someone who: can speak some English; can handle money and people confidently; is warm, open, patient, polite, friendly and helpful, and is flexible about working hours.

Reading about work experience

2 **a** Copy this onto the board:

	past	present	future
Raquel			
Nuria			

Learners read about Raquel and Nuria and make notes under the headings. Check answers.

b Discuss as a class.

Key

2a Raquel: <u>past:</u> worked in another airport shop; did a computing course
<u>present:</u> works for W H Smith; studies to be a stewardess
<u>future:</u> wants to work on planes as a stewardess

Nuria: <u>past:</u> went to England to learn English
<u>present:</u> studies tourism and English; works at W H Smith
<u>future:</u> wants to learn German in Germany, and to work in tourism

Talking point

See note on page 5.

Grammar: *used to*

3 Copy the sentence about Raquel onto the board. Discuss the exercise in pairs or as a class. Then write **Raquel worked in another airport shop** on the board. Discuss the difference in meaning between *used to* and the past simple (*used to* implies that she probably worked there for longer as it was a past routine).

4 Give an example from your own life to demonstrate the task. If you wish, copy these prompts onto the board:

- **home** • **work** • **hobbies** • **appearance**
- **personal qualities** • **clothes**

First learners use them to make notes using *I used to …* and *I didn't use to …* . Then they exchange experiences in pairs. Monitor and correct any errors you hear with *used to*.

Key

3a Yes, she did. **b** No, she doesn't.
c • Did Raquel use to … • Nuria didn't use to …

Extra practice

As an extension, each learner writes three sentences about themselves about things they used / didn't use to do / be: two are true and one is false. In small groups, they take it in turn to read out their sentences. The others ask questions to try to find out which sentence is false.

Listening and Speaking: specialist skills

5 Learners discuss the three questions in pairs and as a class. If you wish, discuss if certain flowers are used for specific occasions in their countries, e.g. for funerals.

6 If you wish, play the tape once for learners to compare what Aileen says with their discussion in Exercise 5. Then play the tape again. Learners do the exercise. Check answers.

Flower deliveries arrive from our wholesaler each Monday and Thursday morning. They come from all over the world and many are imported from the international flower market in Amsterdam. Those two days start with three hectic hours cutting and preparing the flowers, and placing them in water in the cool, dark storeroom.
I've been here for over a year, learning the skills of floristry by working with the shop owner – but there is still a great deal to

learn. It was at least six months before I felt confident enough to deal with the many different questions that customers ask. With ever-changing varieties of plants and flowers to find out about, I may never stop learning.

Floristry involves far more than putting flowers in water. As well as looking after cut flowers and plants we have a workshop to make up bouquets and other displays, and I'm learning how to produce more complex arrangements. We also have a computer terminal for the Interflora orders. Shops throughout the world are linked to the system, and we send and receive many orders each day.

Not all our customers visit us for happy reasons of course, and some come in soon after the death of a relative or close friend. That can sometimes be very distressing. I need to be sympathetic, and try to give them whatever advice they need. Most people working in shops will tell you about those occasional customers who are difficult to serve or not very polite. This happens even in a flower shop, but I must say that meeting the vast majority of customers, both young and old, is the most enjoyable part of each working day.

7 Write the four categories on to the board. Demonstrate the task with *wholesaler*. In pairs, learners categorise the words in the same way. Write their answers on the board. Drill for correct pronunciation. In pairs, learners add two words to each category: if possible, they should be related to a florist's. Use the board to collate their answers.

Key

6 Cutting and preparing flowers; putting them in water; dealing with customers' questions and advising them; learning about the different plants; making up bouquets and displays; sending and receiving Interflora orders.

7a bouquets /buːˈkeɪz/, displays, arrangements, (rose, lily)

b wholesaler (supplier, nursery)

c confident, distressing, sympathetic (upsetting, nervous)

d storeroom, workshop (office, warehouse)

Speaking: an interview

8 In pairs, learners choose a different kind of shop that Aileen worked in before. They read their roles and plan what they are going to say. Then they roleplay their conversations. Note down any errors you hear for correction at the end of the task. For feedback, pairs can roleplay their conversation for the whole class without mentioning the job title: the other learners guess the job.

Grammar backup 3

Past continuous

Key

1b arrived, was raining **c** weren't working, were watching
d Was she sleeping, phoned? wasn't **e** were chatting, was writing **f** arrived **g** sent, replied **h** Did he send

Used to

Key

2b They used **to** drive to work but now they take the train.
c We **didn't** use to work shifts but now we do.
d I **used** to work for an airline office.
e Yes, she **did**.
f I **smoked** for ten years.

At your service

4A Retail strategies

Action

- Interpret signs
- Read a newspaper article
- Express possibilities and certainties
- Grammar: first conditional sentences

Discussion: interpreting signs

1 Check learners understand *departure board* and *boarding*. Discuss the exercise. If necessary, explain *cancelled* and *delayed*. Find out if learners have experienced delays or cancellations at airports and what they did.

2 Establish that the passengers will probably do different things. Learners discuss the exercise in pairs and as a class.

Key

1a Go to Gate 2 immediately to board the plane.
 b Go to the airline desk and ask about alternative arrangements.
 c Find something to do while you wait in the departure lounge for your flight.
2 suggested answers
 a She might work on her lap-top computer.
 b They might have lunch and then play games.
 c They might go to the bar.
 d They might wait in a cafe or look at the shops.

Reading: a newspaper article

3 Find out if learners have been to an international airport and what they thought of the shops. Check learners understand *retailers* and *rents*. They discuss the exercise in pairs and as a class. Do not confirm their answers yet. Then they read the article to see if their ideas were correct.

4 This exercise checks vocabulary from the text. Demonstrate the task: get learners to find *source of income* in the text. Then discuss **a** as a class. Learners do the same for the other expressions. Compare answers in pairs and as a class. Check learners remember the meaning of *to source* from Unit 3. If you wish, ask learners to find *brands, bargain, mall, outlet* in the text. In pairs, they discuss their meaning. Use these questions to check understanding:
 • *What's the name of a brand of toothpaste?*
 • *Who's been to a mall? Which one? What was it like?*
 • *When can you sometimes get a bargain?*
 • *What's the name of a company with a lot of high-street outlets?*

Key

3a Because different goods attract passengers on different flights.
 b Because their income is higher, and is growing much faster, than in the high street.

4a selling shoes **b** tax
 c Clothes that are expensive because they are labelled with the name of a well-known designer.
 d To find out what people want and therefore what goods they will buy and what services they will use.
 e Perfume and Belgian chocolates are luxury items because you can live without them. Examples: fast, expensive cars, expensive jewellery.

Grammar: first conditional sentences

5 Copy the two sentences onto the board. Learners discuss **a** and **b** in pairs or as a class. Use the board to highlight their answers. Then they complete the sentences in **c**. Check answers.

Key

5a The shops will do well.
 b *If* + simple present. *Will* + infinitive.
 c • will go • am / feel, will eat / have • will miss, are / arrive • will ... do, is • Will ... get ... have

Speaking: expressing possibilities and certainties

Copy this onto the board:

If the weather is fine at the weekend, I'll probably ...
 I definitely won't ...
 I might ...
 I'll certainly ...
 I may ...

Learners complete the sentences for themselves. Compare in pairs. Then copy these headings onto the board:
• **100% sure**
• **60% sure**
• **30% sure**
Ask *Which expressions are for 100% sure?* Elicit *I'll certainly, I definitely won't*. Write an example sentence on the board. Do the same for the other headings.

6 Refer learners to the Phrasebook. They discuss **a** and **b** in pairs or as a class. Use the sentences on the board to highlight their answers. Then they complete the sentences in **c**. Check answers.

7 As a class, brainstorm people who travel in groups. Write learners' ideas on the board. In pairs, they choose three of the groups. They discuss what they think each group will / won't buy and what they will put on display. They use the expressions in the Phrasebook to report their decisions to the class. Note down any errors you hear with the target language. Use the board to correct them at the end of the exercise.

Key

6a might, may **b** after will; before won't

Extra practice

P 4.1 Learners work in small groups. Make a photocopy of the worksheet on page 78 for each group and cut it up. Write the order of the cards on the back so learners only turn them over one at a time. Learners share out the situations in their groups. Check they understand *A levels*. Copy this onto the board:

She'll certainly ..., She definitely won't ..., She'll probably ..., She may ..., She might ... .

The first learner reads out the first part of the scenario and the questions. The group discusses what they think will happen, using the language on the board. When they have reached agreement, the second learner reads out the next part. They see if their guesses were correct and then continue in the same way.

4B Around the airport

Action

- **Listen to conversations and announcements**
- **Take part in service transactions**
- **Make requests**
- **Ask for a description**

Listening: conversations and announcements

In pairs, learners list the jobs that people in airports do, e.g. cashier, sales assistant etc. Write all their ideas on the board. Discuss which ones they would / wouldn't like to do and why.

1 In pairs, learners look at the pictures and discuss the questions. Check answers as a class.

2 Write **1–10** on the board. Play the first extract. Ask: *Which picture is it for?* Write **H** next to **1**. Play the other extracts. Check answers.

1 *In green? Size 42? I'll just check for you.*
2 *Please have your passports and boarding passes ready for inspection.*
3 *Would Mr Pirelli, travelling to Rome on flight IB 487, please go immediately to Gate 16.*
4 *Can you open that green case, please? Thank you. So where have you just come from?*
5 *Did you pack your bags yourself? Good. And have they been with you at all times?*
6 *That's 550 pesetas for the coffees. Would you like anything else?*
7 *Right. Could you give me a detailed description of the bag and its contents. What colour is the suitcase?*
8 *Right. There are seats available at 2.00 and 4.30. When would you like to travel?*
9 *Yes, we do charge commission on traveller's cheques. Our rates are on the board here.*
10 *Would you mind moving away from the entrance, please?*

3 a Learners look at the pictures again and discuss the questions. Check as a class. Do not worry if they do not know all the answers. They will listen to the tape again in **c**.
b and c Demonstrate the task with *charge commission*. Learners discuss the exercise in pairs. Play the tape again to check answers for **b** and **c**.

Key

1a and b

A A customs official (who checks people's bags to make sure there is nothing illegal in them); in the custom's area / hall.
B A member of the airport staff (who makes public announcements); in an administrative office.
C An airport official (who deals with complaints about lost luggage); in the baggage collection hall.
D A member of the airline staff (who checks in passengers and their luggage); at a check-in desk.
E A member of the airline staff (who checks the tickets of people boarding a plane); in the departure lounge, at the boarding gate.
F A security guard (who is responsible for the security and safety of passengers and the airport); at the entrance to the airport.
G A cashier (who changes money); at the desk of an exchange bureau.
H A shop assistant (who serves customers); in a boutique / clothes shop.
I A waiter (who serves food and drinks); in a cafe.
J A member of the airline staff (who sells and changes tickets); at a ticket sales desk.
  d Arriving: A, C   Leaving: D, E, H, I, J   Either: F, G
2 1H, 2E, 3B, 4A, 5D, 6I, 7C, 8J, 9G, 10F

3a

A The green one.
B Gate 16.
C A description of the lost bag and its contents.
D The passenger did.
E They are boarding the plane.
F He wants the family to move away from the entrance.
G To change some traveller's cheques.
H A blouse.
I 275 pesetas.
J At 2.00 or 4.30.
  b charge commission – G; boarding passes – E; a detailed description – C; pack your bags – D; please go immediately – B; anything else – I; the entrance – F; seats available – J; check for you – H; that green case – A

Speaking: service transactions

Copy these sentences onto the board.

- .... have your passports ready.
- .... Mr Pirelli .... go immediately to Gate 16.
- .... you .... that green case, please?
- .... you .... me a description?
- **When .... you like to travel?**
- .... you mind .... away from the entrance?

In pairs, learners see if they can complete the sentences. Play the extracts again for them to check their answers. Drill the requests for correct stress and intonation. Then direct learners do the requests in the Phrasebook: write them on the board next to the ones with the same form. Drill again as necessary.

4 In pairs, learners choose three pictures. Make sure they do not choose B or E. Refer them to the expressions in the Phrasebook. They use them to roleplay their conversations. For feedback, volunteer pairs can roleplay their conversations. Finally, use the board to correct any errors you heard.

Speaking: asking for a description

5 Learners discuss the exercise in pairs and as a class.

6 Learners complete the questions. Check answers.

7 First each learner completes the lost luggage form. Then divide them into pairs. They read their roles and take it in turns to roleplay the conversation. Follow the same procedure for feedback as Exercise 4.

Key

5a It's a suitcase. **b** It's one metre long. **c** It's half a metre wide.
d It's black. **e** It weighs 22 kilos.
What + noun; *how* + adjective.
6a how **b** how **c** what **d** how **e** what

Extra practice

Each learner uses the questions in Exercise 5 to write a short description of an object. They must not mention the name of the object. In groups, they each read out their description. The other learners guess what it is.

4C The personal touch

Action

- **Read a newspaper article**
- **Change money**
- **Listen to a conversation at an exchange desk**
- **Vocabulary: currencies and financial words**

Reading: a newspaper article

Write the items from the article on the board. Discuss where people normally buy them, e.g. maggots from pet shop.

1 Learners discuss the exercise in pairs or as a class.

2 Learners read the article and list the things that you can buy from a vending machine. Then they discuss the exercise in pairs or as a class. Find out what vending machines sell in their countries and where they can find them.

3 Write **a–i** on the board. Ask learners to find *common* in the text. Discuss what it means and write the missing word from the definition on the board. Learners complete the other definitions in the same way. Check answers.

Key

1a A machine that sells things.
b People eat pizza. Fish eat maggots.
3a unusual **b** dead **c** real **d** throw it away
e small, quick **f** flowers **g** patients / sick people
h dirty **i** go bad

Speaking: machine transactions

4 Learners look at the picture and discuss the exercise in pairs and as a class. Find out if they have ever used currency exchange machines.

Key

4a It changes money of one currency to another.
b You put in foreign currency bank notes; the machine automatically exchanges them for the currency of the country you are visiting.
c notes.
d You can get money at any time; it's quick. But you can't change all currencies; it runs out of money; it could be dangerous to change large amounts of money. It cannot tell you the current exchange rate.

Vocabulary: currencies

5 Copy this chart onto the board:

currency	country	nationality
pound	UK, Ireland	British, Irish

In pairs, learners decide which countries use which currencies and if you wish, the nationality of each country. Write their answers on the board. Drill for correct pronunciation as necessary. In pairs, learners add other currencies to their charts. Check as a class.

Key

5 pound – UK, Ireland, Egypt, Cyprus; peso – Argentina, Mexico, Chile, Colombia, Cuba; franc – France, Belgium, Switzerland; dollar – USA, Canada, Australia; yen – Japan; mark – Germany; rouble – Russia; escudo – Portugal; peseta – Spain; yuan – China; krona – Sweden; lira – Italy, Turkey.

Talking point

See note on page 5.

Speaking and Listening: changing money

6 Direct learners to the eight pictures. Discuss what is happening in each picture. Then in pairs, learners write the conversation and practise it. Play the conversation for learners to compare it with theirs. In pairs, learners roleplay a similar conversation using their own currency. For feedback, volunteer pairs roleplay their conversations for the whole class.

(A = cashier   B = customer)
A: *Good morning. Can I help you?*
B: *I'd like to change some dollar traveller's cheques into pesetas, please.*
A: *Fine. How much would you like to change?*
B: *Er ... What's the rate for the dollar today?*
A: *It's 127 pesetas.*
B: *Right. I see. Um ... I'll just change a hundred dollars, then, please.*
A: *A hundred. OK. Could you sign each cheque there, please?*
B: *Right.*
A: *And can I see your passport, please?*
B: *Yes, certainly. Here you are.*
A: *Here you are. And your receipt. We take 2% commission, so that's 12,446 pesetas.*
B: *Er – so what's this coin here?*
A: *It's a hundred pesetas – that's about eighty cents.*
B: *Right. Thank you very much.*
A: *Thank you.*

23

Grammar backup 4

First conditional sentences

Key
1b 'll pay, get
 c will get, decides
 d doesn't arrive, 'll go
 e don't go, won't get
 f finish, won't get
2b I'll go sailing if the weather is good at the weekend.
 c What will they do if the sound system doesn't arrive?
 d If we don't phone them immediately, we'll lose the contract.
 e If he likes the vase, he'll buy it.

Sound check

Note: These exercises can be used at any stage of the Course Book.

Word stress

Same spelling, different stress

1 Copy the two sentences in the exercise onto the board. Learners listen to the tape and read the sentences. Discuss what part of speech *export* is in each sentence and how the stress on *export* changes and why.

 export – Asian companies export a lot of electronic goods to Europe.
 export – Japanese exports to Europe are very high.

2 In pairs, learners discuss the meaning of the words. Then they practise saying them as nouns and then as verbs. Play the tape for them to check their answers. If you wish, play the tape again, pausing after each pair of words for the learners to repeat.

 import, import; increase, increase; decrease, decrease; transport, transport; contract, contract; produce, produce; extract, extract; insult, insult; progress, progress; contrast, contrast; transfer, transfer; record, record

3 Each learner writes three sentences using the words in Exercise 2. In pairs, they take it in turns to read their sentences to their partner who checks that the stress on the noun / verb is correct.

Key
1 verb, noun

No stress

To introduce the idea of the schwa [ə], write your name (or one of the learner's names) on the board. Underline the [ə] and elicit how you say it. Learners then identify the [ə] sound in other learners' names.

1 Learners look at the words and listen to the tape.

 manager, worker, shopper, wholesaler, carton, system

2 Learners repeat the words in pairs or as a class.

3 Copy the words in the exercise onto the board. In pairs, learners say the words and underline the /ə/ sounds.

4 Play the tape for learners to check their answers. Underline the [ə] sounds on the board. Drill for correct pronunciation.

 attend, assistant, confirm, recommend, accurate, seasonal

Key
3 att**e**nd, **a**ssist**a**nt, c**o**nfirm, rec**o**mmend, accur**a**te, seas**o**nal

Prefixes and suffixes

1 Copy the words in the exercise onto the board. Check learners understand *prefix* and *suffix*. Learners look at the words and listen to the tape.
 a Learners mark the main stress on each word. Check answers on the board.
 b Discuss as a class.

 impatient, inflexible, uneconomic, distasteful, impossible

2 Copy the words onto the board. In pairs, learners say the words and mark the stress. Play the tape for them to check their answers. Together, mark the stress on the board.

 untidily, improbable, uncommonly, unsympathetic, disagreeable, disappearance

Key
1a im'patient, in'flexible, uneco'nomic, dis'tasteful, im'possible
 b no

5 On show

5A An international exhibition

Action

- **Talk about exhibitions**
- **Listen to an interview**
- **Write a follow-up letter**
- **Vocabulary: exhibitions**
- **Grammar: revision of tenses**

Speaking: exhibitions

1 Learners look at the photographs and discuss the questions. If you wish, discuss the advantages and disadvantages of having a stand at such event, e.g. *it's expensive but you meet a lot of potential clients* etc.

2 Learners discuss the exercise in pairs and as a class.

Key

1a 9th–13th February, at Earls Court in London.
 b An international exhibition of food and drink.
2a • An exhibitor pays for a stand.
  • Samples are usually free to customers; the exhibitor pays the costs of providing them.
 b • You watch someone demonstrating something.
  • You taste samples of food and drink.
 c • Because the price is lower than usual. If you get a discount, money is taken off the display price of the object.
  • A promotion usually involves a special price for goods or a lower price if you buy a certain quantity.
 d • A buyer negotiates to get the lowest possible price.
  • Companies sponsor events to publicise the name of their organisation and to be linked with the success of a particular event.

Listening and Reading: an interview

3 Learners discuss the questions in small groups. Compare ideas as a class but do not confirm their ideas yet. Next they listen to and read the interview. Check answers.

There are over a thousand exhibitors here from all parts of the world. Most of the big international food and drink companies have taken a stand, and a lot of small ones too. This is a trade exhibition – it's not for members of the public. Manufacturers come here to meet buyers from other companies. It gives buyers and sellers a chance to get to know each other. Exhibitors have brought their new products here, and most of them are doing special promotions to encourage people to buy them. A lot of business is done because everybody knows you can negotiate good discounts. There are lots of events too. Earlier today there was a dragon dance sponsored by a Chinese company, and at midday a West Indian band is playing at the Caribbean food stand. And at a show like this, you don't pay for lunch! Lots of companies are doing cooking demonstrations and tastings, so there are plenty of free samples. It's an important event for anyone in the food industry. Last year's exhibition was very successful, and this year is even better.

Key

3a Buyers from companies that do business in the food and drink trade.
 b Large and small food and drink companies that are exhibiting their products.
 c Through special promotions, discounts, samples, demonstrations and other events.
 d Because it is a chance to meet buyers personally and to do business face to face.

Vocabulary: exhibitions

4 Copy the chart onto the board. Learners find the words in the interview and complete the chart. Check answers and establish which nouns refer to people.

Key

4
verb	noun	verb	noun
exhibit	exhibition / exhibitor	demonstrate	demonstration
sample	sample	taste	tasting
promote	promotion	sell	seller
buy	buyer	manufacture	manufacturer

Exhibitor, buyer, seller and manufacturer refer to people.

Grammar: revision of tenses

5 Copy the sentences onto the board so that you have all six examples, e.g.:

Most companies | have taken / took | a stand.

Learners discuss the exercise in pairs or as a class. Use the sentences on the board to highlight their answers.

Key

5a *have taken:* present perfect simple; a non-specific (recent) time in the past
  come: present simple; a general truth about a routine
  was playing: past continuous; a period of time in the past, which started before 11 o'clock and continued after 11 o'clock
 b *took:* past simple; a specific time in the past
  are coming: present continuous; happening at the time of speaking or planned for the future
  played: past simple; in the past, started at 11 o'clock (not before)
 c • *present activities:* present simple, present continuous
  past activities: present perfect simple, past continuous, past simple
  • *future activities:* present continuous
 d Most companies haven't taken / didn't take a stand.
  Manufacturers don't come / aren't coming here to meet buyers.
  A West Indian band wasn't playing / didn't play at 11 o'clock.
  past simple – did; present simple – do.

Extra practice

P 5.1 Photocopy the *Find someone who ...!* questionnaire on page 79. Learners mingle and interview each other.

Reading and Writing: a follow-up letter

Ask learners questions about the letter, e.g. *Who is the letter to?* *Which company is it from?* etc. Establish where the addresses, date and names go and if you wish, compare the layout of the letter in the exercise with the layout learners use at work. Discuss why the letter ends *Yours sincerely* (it begins with *Dear* + name), and how you end a letter if you don't know the person's name (*Yours faithfully*). If you wish, find out if learners use other phrases in a follow-up letter.

6 Learners read the letter and then read the enquiry card. They write their reply. For feedback, learners read out the first part of their letters. As a class, decide the best version and write it on the board to provide a model answer.

> **Key**
>
> **suggested answer**
>
> Caribbean International Ltd
> George Avenue
> Norwich NR5 4ST
> (Date)
>
> Mr Beckett
> JB Supermarkets
> JB House
> Crown Square
> Cambridge CB3 8KM
>
> Dear Mr Beckett
> Thank you for your enquiry about Caribbean International fruit juices and fruit snack bars.
> I enclose information on these products. If you would like to discuss any aspect of our products and pricing, please contact me at the above address and I can arrange to call on you at your convenience.
> I look forward to hearing from you.
>
> Yours sincerely
>
> Jennifer Briton
>
> Jennifer Briton
> Sales Manager

5B Good taste

Action

- **Read about a company**
- **Listen to a conversation**
- **Describe personal responses**
- **Vocabulary: business activities, emphasising adverbs, responses to food**

Reading: introducing a company

1 Find out if learners have heard of Neuhaus and what they know about it. They read the texts and answer the questions. Check answers.

> **Key**
>
> **1a** • Neuhaus.
> • Belgium.
> • Marketing Manager.
> **b** • Belgian chocolates and chocolate related products.
> • Three.
> • To meet distributors, retailers, buyers from stores and supermarkets and catering contractors who may be interested in their products.
> **c** • It started in 1857.
> • It is the oldest chocolate house in Belgium; it created the Praline, and it is still one of the most innovative chocolate houses.

Vocabulary: business activities

2 Write **a–e** on the board. Learners read the texts again to find the words for the definitions. Write their answers on the board. Drill for correct stress.

> **Key**
>
> **2a** retailers **b** buyers **c** distributors
> **d** catering contractors

Listening to a conversation

3 **a** Learners describe what is happening in the photograph. Discuss what they think the man is saying.
b Play the tape. Learners note down what the man likes about the chocolate. Check answers.

> (K = Karine   S = Stephen)
> K: *This is one of our most famous chocolates. It's called 'Caprice'.*
> S: *'Caprice'?*
> K: *Yes, the filling is made with fresh cream and it's covered with dark chocolate. We sell a lot of Caprice. It's very popular.*
> S: *Well, it looks beautiful. It's a very unusual shape.*
> K: *Yes, we try to make our chocolates look beautiful as well as tasting beautiful. Why don't you taste it?*
> S: *Mmm ... oh yes ... mmm.*
> K: *What do you think?*
> S: *Oh ... it's wonderful ... absolutely delicious ... and it tastes so creamy.*

4 Copy this onto the board:

It looks ....

It's ......, absolutely ....

It tastes so ....

Learners listen again and answer **a** and **b**. Write their answers to **b** on the board.
c Discuss as a class.
d Learners discuss the exercise in pairs. Write their answers on the board. Leave them there for Exercise 5.

Key

3a The man is tasting a chocolate at the Neuhaus stand.
 b He likes the creamy taste.
4a It's made from dark chocolate and fresh cream.
 b It looks beautiful. It's a very unusual shape, absolutely delicious, and it tastes so creamy.
 c really, quite

Vocabulary: responses to food

5 Learners look at the chart. Demonstrate the task: ask *Which words under 'General' are negative?* In pairs, learners categorise the adjectives in the same way. Check as a class, drilling for correct pronunciation as necessary. Refer learners to their words from Exercise 4. They write them in the appropriate column and categorise them in the same way. See if they can add any other words. Check as a class. If you wish, elicit examples of the kinds of food that the adjectives under 'taste' can describe, e.g. *stale bread, sweet chocolate*.

Key

5 terrible, awful, unpleasant, unattractive, disgusting, foul, stale, bitter (sometimes)

Vocabulary: emphasising adverbs

6 Books closed. Write the adverbs onto the board:
 absolutely / simply / really + ...
 really / very / extremely + ...
 Add any others the learners had from Exercise 4. Ask *Which adverbs can you use with boring?* Write **boring** after **really / very / extremely** on the board. Do the same with the other adjectives in the exercise. Establish when the different adverbs are used. Drill for correct pronunciation. Ask two learners to read out the example exchange. In pairs, they practise similar exchanges using the prompts and the words in the chart. Note down any errors you hear. For feedback, volunteer pairs can roleplay their exchanges for the whole class. Use the board to correct any errors you heard at the end of the exercise.

7 Copy the two sentences onto the board. Discuss the question. Highlight learners' answers on the board. Elicit other verbs of the senses (*looks, sounds, smells, feels*) and write them on the board.

Key

7 It tastes + adjective; It tastes like + noun.

Speaking: personal responses

8 Check learners understand the expressions in the Phrasebook. In pairs, they discuss their responses to the pictures, using the expressions in the Phrasebook and the adjectives and adverbs in Exercises 5 and 6. Compare responses as a class.

Extra practice

Learners work in small groups. They each think of one thing: it can be food, a restaurant / place they know. They describe the thing to the others using the vocabulary in Exercises 5, 6 and the Phrasebook. They must not say what it is. The others have to guess what they're describing, e.g. *I ate this absolutely delicious ... yesterday. It tasted sweet and nutty and although it looked unattractive, it wasn't. (A new breakfast cereal.)*

5C Best buys

Action

- Talk about specifications
- Read promotional signs
- Listen to a conversation
- Make a sale
- Grammar: comparisons and degrees of difference

Speaking: specifications

Find out if learners have a computer at work or home. Discuss what they like and dislike about it.

1 Check learners understand *portable* and the qualities in the box. In pairs, they discuss the exercise. Compare ideas as a class.

Reading promotional signs

2 Ask a learner to read out the first sign. Discuss the two questions as a class. Follow the same procedure with the other signs.

3 Check learners understand *hard disk*. Learners look at the chart in Exercise 5. In pairs, they decide if the statements are true or false. Check as a class.

Key

2a No, there aren't.   **b** as fast as   **c** considerably lighter
 d No, it doesn't.   **e** less expensive
3a False. The PACEMAKER is the most expensive machine.
 b False. The GATE is lighter than the PIXEL.
 c True.   **d** True.   **e** True.

Grammar: comparisons

4 **a** Copy the chart onto the board. Learners complete it using the information in Exercises 2 and 3. Check answers.
 b and c Learners complete the gaps. Check answers. Elicit the rules of how to form comparative and superlative adjectives. Highlight the spelling changes: final *y* changes to *i* +*er/est*; one syllable adjectives which end with a vowel + consonant, the final consonant is doubled.

5 If possible, bring two objects (or pictures of objects) into class which are similar, e.g. a glossy travel book and a novel. First learners read the sentences in the Phrasebook. Then compare your objects in the same way, e.g. *This book is a little shorter, it's a lot cheaper, much more interesting, far heavier, considerably more useful.*

Learners do the exercise in pairs: make sure they use the expressions in the Phrasebook. Alternatively, tell each pair that they are going to 'sell' their portable to the rest of the class.

Each pair chooses one of the portables to write their sentences about. They read out their sentences and say why people should buy theirs. The pair with the best sentences sells the most!

Key

4a

adjective	comparative	superlative
light	lighter	the lightest
expensive	more expensive	the most expensive
cheap	cheaper	the cheapest
powerful	more powerful	the most powerful
heavy	heavier	the heaviest
short	shorter	the shortest
big	bigger	the biggest

b cheaper; cheap; the cheapest

c more powerful; powerful; the most powerful

Extra practice

1 Copy some prompts onto pieces of paper, one for each pair of learners, e.g.
- learning English / Chinese / German
- driving to work / walking to work / taking the train to work
- going on a trekking holiday / going on a beach holiday / going on a sightseeing holiday
- writing letters / using e-mail / sending faxes
  Learners write three or four sentences comparing their prompts, e.g. *Learning English is much more difficult than learning German.* Then they mingle and find out how many learners agree with their sentences.

P 5.2 **2** This activity revises the vocabulary from Action A and making comparisons. Make one photocopy of the worksheet on page 79 for each group. Tell the learners that they work for a company which produces crisps and snacks. They have just developed a new kind of crisp, 'the Crispette', which is a small crisp / biscuit that you have with a drink. Their promotion budget is £50,000 and they are going to have a meeting to decide how to spend the money. They can have one 'free' idea as long as the other learners don't think it is unreasonable! Check they understand *reply / tear-off slip* and *mailshot*. The learners work in small groups and discuss how they are going to spend the money. They report their decisions to the other learners.

Listening and Speaking: making a sale

6 Learners listen to the conversation and answer the questions. Check answers.

(S = salesperson   C = customer)

s: *Can I help you? Or are you just looking?*

c: *Er ... well ... I'm looking for a portable.*

s: *I see. And have you looked at any other machines at the exhibition?*

c: *Well ... yes, I'm quite impressed by the GATE 166, so I wanted to compare it with this one.*

s: *Our 166? OK. Well. It's our best-selling machine. It's battery or mains-operated and the battery life is longer than any other machine in its price range – over six hours.*

c: *Right ... the battery life in the GATE is as long as that.*

s: *Right ... er ...*

c: *What about the hard disk? How big is the hard disk?*

s: *It comes with a one gigabyte hard disk as standard. It's our fastest machine. It's got a 166 chip in it, as the name suggests.*

c: *But what about the weight. How heavy is it?*

s: *Oh, it's very light. Only three and a half kilos.*

c: *Right. The GATE machine is lighter, then.*

s: *Yes, just a little, but we're doing a special offer for anyone who buys at the exhibition ... two years' free maintenance and support.*

c: *Two years ... right. That sounds good.*

s: *And nobody can beat our price. It's the least expensive machine available with these specifications, at only £1750.*

c: *Oh ... but isn't the GATE cheaper? They're giving a ten per cent discount for people buying at the exhibition.*

s: *I see. Well, if you decide to buy our machine, I'm sure we can match their price.*

7 Divide half the class into **A**s and half into **B**s. They read their roles. Together the **A**s discuss their arguments and the **B**s brainstorm the questions they will ask. Monitor and help. Then divide learners into **A** and **B** pairs. They roleplay their conversation. Note down any errors you hear. For feedback, find out which salespeople were successful and why. Finally correct errors. If you wish, learners can change roles: the **B**s try to persuade the **A**s to buy the Gate 166.

Key

6a the Pixel 166   **b** the customer   **c** £1,620

Grammar backup 5

Revision of tenses

Key

1b is writing   **c** am meeting   **d** haven't arrived
  e Did she visit   **f** have met   **g** has lived
2b have had   **c** Have you seen   **d** was sending
  e have bought   **f** have attended   **g** are living

Comparative and superlative adjectives, *as* + adj + *as*

Key

1b wetter, wettest   **c** spicier, spiciest
  d more incredible, most incredible   **e** safer, safest
  f sweeter, sweetest   **g** worse, worst
2b more expensive   **c** lighter   **d** more attractive   **e** big as
  f cheaper   **g** more convenient   **h** closer   **i** better ... than

6 On the market

6A Neuhaus Mondose

Action

- **Read an introduction to a company**
- **Vocabulary: compound words**
- **Grammar: defining relative clauses**

Reading: an introduction to a company

1 Learners discuss the questions in pairs and as a class.

2 Check learners understand *invent*, *filling* and *shell*. Learners read the article and answer the questions. Check answers. Check the pronunciation of almond /ˈɑːmənd/.

3 Read out **a** and get learners to finish the definition. Learners do the same with the other words. Check answers. Establish the difference in meaning between *loose* /luːs/, *to lose* /luːz/ and *a loss* /lɒs/.

Key

2a In 1857, in the centre of Brussels.
 b The praline; chocolates with rich fillings covered by a chocolate shell; and the ballotin.
 c Europe, the United States, Japan.
 d Ballotins (packaging for chocolates); a chocolate shell and its filling; almonds.
3a A confectioner makes or sells sweets.
 b A damaged item is broken or of poor quality.
 c Packaging protects a product.
 d A loose chocolate can move freely in its container.
 e A company's turnover is the amount of business it does.
 f A company's main market is the place where it sells most.
 g A department store sells a wide variety of goods.

Vocabulary: compound words

4 Copy the three example compound words onto the board. Discuss what they mean. Compare their ideas with the definitions in the exercise. Write **a–f** on the board. Learners write the compound words. Compare answers in pairs and write them on the board. Establish that the stress is on the first word and that no hyphen is needed with compounds formed with *wide*. See if learners can think of any other examples, e.g. *lead-free, countrywide, man-made*.

Key

4a factory-made **b** sugar-free **c** nationwide
 d Europewide **e** rent-free **f** machine-made

Grammar: defining relative clauses

5 Copy the two example sentences onto the board. Discuss the exercise in pairs or as a class. Use the board to highlight answers to **c** and **e**.

6 Copy the three headings onto the board. Ask learners to read the text again to find the first defining relative clause. They read it out. Write **that** next to **things**. Use the same procedure to find the other relative pronouns.

7 Learners complete the sentences. Check answers.

8 First complete the three sentences about yourself. Read them out to the class with your reasons. Then learners complete the sentences for themselves. In small groups, they discuss their ideas. Correct any errors you hear with defining relative clauses.

Key

5a No, there isn't. **b** No, it isn't. **c** The company.
 d No, they aren't. **e** The markets.
6a who **b** where **c** that / which
7a that / which **b** who **c** that / which
 d where **e** that / which

Extra practice

P 6.1 This activity revises vocabulary from Units 1–6 and practises defining relative clauses. Photocopy the two crosswords on page 80. Write the beginnings of these definitions on the board:
This is a place where …
This is something that / which …
This is when …
This is someone who …
Learners work in pairs: one has an **A** crossword, one has a **B** crossword. They take it in turns to define the missing words e.g. *Four across is something that you look at to find a product* (a catalogue).

6B Products

Action

- **Listen to a description of a product range**
- **Describe objects and products**
- **Listen to an interview**
- **Vocabulary: containers, shapes**

Vocabulary: containers

1 First learners discuss **a** and **b** in pairs. Compare answers. Copy the containers onto the board, e.g. **a barrel of …** . List two more things that can be stored in each container. Discuss **c** as a class.

Key

1a bag: paper, plastic   barrel: wood, metal
box: cardboard, wood   carton: cardboard
jar: glass, plastic   packet: paper, cardboard
sack: cloth, plastic   tin: metal
tube: plastic, metal, paper, cardboard

b suggested answers
bag of crisps, barrel of beer, box of chocolates, carton of orange juice, jar of jam, packet of tea, sack of potatoes, tin of soup, tube of toothpaste

c boxes, packets, tins

Listening to a description of a product range

2 Refer learners back to the pictures at the top of the page. Play the interview until '*500 grams*'. Elicit which picture she is talking about. Play the rest of the interview for the learners to sequence the pictures. Check answers.

We sell loose chocolates in different sizes of ballotin – they are sold by weight, for example, 250 grams, 500 grams. Then we sell a range of boxes of chocolates – our Opera collection is very popular – and a selection of tins. These are decorated ... we have the 1900, the Garden. And we also make napolitains – small flat squares of chocolate that people often eat with a cup of coffee. And of course we make bars of chocolate, we make a lot of different types. We also produce a very small box, or packet, with just two chocolates in it. These are usually sold to catering companies or hotels and airlines who put their own name on the side.

3 Learners listen to the interview again and answer the questions.

Key

2 boxes, tins, packet
3a They are sold by weight.
b D
c A

Vocabulary: shapes

4 a In pairs, learners label the shapes. For feedback, draw the shapes on the board. Label them as a class. Drill for correct pronunciation.
b In pairs learners look at the pictures in the exercise and on page 48 and find the shapes. Check as a class.

5 Demonstrate the task: draw an L-shaped room on the board. Learners then do the same for the other objects. Compare drawings in pairs.

6 Read out the first description. Learners guess the object. Then do the same with **b**. Highlight the form **to be made of + material** on the board.

Key

6a a ruler   **b** gloves

Speaking: describing objects

7 Each learner thinks of an object. They write a short description like the ones in Exercise 6. Then they read out their description, stopping after each sentence for the learners to guess. If you wish, make this into a team game.

Listening to an interview

8 Learners discuss the questions in pairs or as a class. The first question prepares them for the first part of the interview; the second question refers to the second part.

9 First learners read the exercise. Then they listen to the tape. They correct the false sentences in **a** and make notes for **b**. Check answers.

The customers who buy in our own shops and in the department stores are mainly women. But in duty-free shops, more and more it's men – people travelling on business. The age of our customers is a little high at the moment. We are obviously targeting people on a good income. City people, people who eat out a lot. At twenty you can't really afford to do that. Now we want to focus on younger people – twenty-five to thirty. We already have a lot of customers around thirty-five to forty, but our main buyers are over fifty.

10 Write the seven nationalities on the board. Learners listen to the second part of the interview and match the nationalities and chocolates. Check answers. Finally compare their ideas from Exercise 8 with what Karine said.

People in different countries like their chocolates in different ways. In Germany they like big chocolates; in Britain it's white chocolates that are not too big. In the US the bigger a chocolate is, the better – local US chocolate makers make very big chocolates. In Britain and Europe people want to buy a box of chocolates. In Japan you buy them individually. In Germany you don't buy wrapped luxury chocolates because for Germans wrapped chocolates are cheap – they are not high quality. In our shop in Harrods in London, Arabs ask us to wrap every chocolate individually.
In countries like France and Germany a lot of customers like very dark, bitter chocolates, with a very high percentage of cacao. We introduced the Yucatan for them – a chocolate with 69% cacao and less sugar and milk. In Britain people aren't interested in dark, bitter chocolates. They like chocolates sweet, with a lot of milk.

Key

9a • False. The main buyers in duty-free shops are men.
   • True. • True.
   • False. The company wants to sell more to 25–30 year olds.
b Older, wealthy people; people who eat in restaurants.
10 Europeans: in boxes
Germans: big, unwrapped, dark and bitter; Americans: big; Japanese: individual; Arabs: individual, wrapped; Britons: white, sweet and milky; in boxes; French: dark and bitter

Speaking and Writing: describing a product

11 a In pairs, learners choose a food or drink product. They discuss the products and make notes under the headings in the exercise.

b They write a description of their product, without mentioning its name. For feedback, pairs swap their descriptions. They guess the kind / name of the product and correct any errors they find.

6C Market research

Action

- **Talk about market research**
- **Interpret data**
- **Explain changes**
- **Vocabulary: fast food outlets, verbs used to describe changes**

Speaking: market research

1 Learners discuss the exercise in pairs and as a class. Discuss different ways of carrying out market research, e.g. street interviews, telephone interviews, questionnaires, government statistics. Find out if learners have ever taken part in any market research. Ask them to give details.

Key

1a Market research investigates people's spending habits. It helps a business to sell more products by marketing them more effectively.

b suggested answers
What age groups will buy the product? How much are they prepared to pay? What features should the product have? What is already available on the market?

Reading and Speaking: interpreting data

2 Direct learners to the table and pictures. Discuss the exercise as a class.

3 Copy these drawings onto the board:

Learners look at the Phrasebook. Elicit which drawing represents each sentence. Check learners know the past simple and past participle of *rise, fall, grow, shrank* and *got*. Remind learners that *gotten* is American English. Then copy this onto the board:

steadily	dramatically	gradually
slightly	sharply	very little

Sales rose ....

Learners look at the arrows and write the adverbs in the order of size / rate of increase.

a First learners read the three sentences in the exercise. Direct them to the prompts. Elicit a statement about Indian food. Then they use the Phrasebook to write similar sentences. Compare answers in pairs and as a class.
b Find out if the trends are similar in their countries. Discuss which kinds of fast food are most popular and if the kinds have changed over the last five years.

4 Learners discuss the exercise in pairs. Compare ideas as a class. Discuss what kind of fast food restaurant they would open in their country.

Key

2a Food that you can buy and eat quickly.
b Hamburger bars, fish and chip shops, pizzerias, sandwich bars, kebab shops.
c Yes, they did.
d No, sandwich bars, bakeries, and cafes sold the most fast food. Hamburger bars and pizzerias also sold more.
3 • Indian take-away food sales increased slightly in 1995.
• The market for fish and chips remained at the same level in 1993.
• The market for pizzas expanded between 1991 and 1995.
• Hamburger sales rose slightly in 1995.
• Total fast food sales grew steadily between 1991 and 1995.

Speaking and Listening: explaining changes

5 Find out how many of the learners' female relatives or friends work. Then discuss why the changing roles of women have led to the increased popularity of fast food. Learners then discuss the exercise in pairs and as a class.

6 Play the first speaker. Elicit which reason he uses from the list in Exercise 5. Play the other speakers for learners to identify the reasons in the same way. Check answers.

(I = Interviewer   C = Consumer)
I: *So why do you eat a lot of fast food, then?*
C: *Oh, because I leave for work at 7 in the morning and don't get home until about 8 at night. So I often pick up something to eat on the way home ...*
I: *And what about you, madam?*
C: *Well, we never seem to be at home at the same times on weekdays. When I get back the children have already gone out. They'll get a sandwich or something if I'm not there ...*
I: *And why do you eat fast food?*
C: *Because I live alone and I don't want to spend time cooking for myself ...*
I: *And you, sir?*
C: *Er ... because it's quite cheap ... and fast-food places often welcome children and families ... we can all eat out together ... and there are no complaints from the children ...*
I: *And what are your reasons?*
C: *I simply haven't got time to cook. If we're not eating fast food from a restaurant, we're probably eating something similar at home ...*

Key

5 suggested answers

a More women work outside the home and they have less time to cook.

b People eating at different times (because of hobbies, different work patterns etc.) are more likely to buy fast food.

c A long working day leaves little time and energy to prepare and cook food when you get home. People buy fast food to eat on the way home.

d Single people often feel that it is too much trouble to cook for one person.

e Advertising persuades children that fast food is delicious, so they ask for it.

6 1c 2b 3d 4e 5a

Listening and Writing: interpreting data

7 Use this table to review the language to interpret data.

verbs ↗	verbs ↘	verbs →	adverbs

Learners complete the table. Check as a class on the board.

a Learners discuss the exercise in pairs or as a class.

b Learners write sentences in pairs. For feedback, they read out their sentences. The others decide if they agree.

Key

7a Sales of tea and coffee fell steadily between 1984 and 1994. Sales of soft drinks rose in the same period.

Extra practice

In small groups, learners use the language from this unit to discuss trends in their countries, e.g. in unemployment, population, number of homeless people, etc.

Grammar backup 6

Defining relative clauses

Key

1b That is the man who I met at a conference last week.

c This is the office which / that I moved into last month.

d I'm sure this is (the street) where I parked my car this morning.

e I have a friend whose boss speaks ten languages.

2b Let's go to that Spanish restaurant **where** the staff are so helpful.

c I always listen to people **whose** ideas are good.

d I remember the time **when** the company made a loss.

e I like people **who / that** are sympathetic.

f This is the awful tablecloth **that / which** I bought on holiday.

g I like people **who are** friendly.

3b The staff who work in central London often have long journeys to work.

c The faxes which arrived yesterday contain very important information.

d The holiday (that) they've just booked is very expensive.

e The meal (that) we had last night was delicious.

f This is the tourist agency where I booked my ticket.

Sound check

Sounds and spelling

Silent letters

1 Direct learners to the words in the chart. Check they understand *comb*, *bomb* and *limb*. Play the tape for them to repeat the words. In pairs, they decide which letters are silent. Check as a class.

🔊 *(k)now, (k)nife, (k)nee, (k)nock*
(w)rite, (w)rong, (w)rap, type(w)riter
campai(g)n, forei(g)n, si(g)n, champa(g)ne
wou(l)d, cou(l)d, shou(l)d, ca(l)m, ta(l)k, wa(l)k
com(b), lam(b), bom(b), lim(b)
li(gh)t, wei(gh), strai(gh)t, throu(gh)

2 In pairs, learners take it in turns to say the words. Find out if learners can think of any more words they know with silent letters.

Words with *ough*

1 Learners practise saying the words in pairs. Check they understand *cough*, *fought*, *rough* and *tough*. Play the tape for them to listen and repeat.

🔊 A *through*
B *although, though*
C *cough*
D *bought, thought, fought, nought*
E *rough, tough, enough*

2 Demonstrate the task: ask *Which word or words have the same sound as in off?* Elicit *cough*. In pairs, learners do the same with the other vowel sounds. Check as a class.

Key

2a cough **b** thought, bought, fought, nought
  c through **d** although, though **e** rough, tough, enough

'Missing' syllables

1 Copy the words in the exercise onto the board. Play the first word. Underline which sound disappears: **bus̲i̲ness**. Play the other words for learners to do the same. Check answers.

🔊 *bus̲i̲ness, inte̲resting, diffe̲rent, choco̲late, tempe̲rature, frighte̲ning*

2 Mark the stress on the board as a class.

3 In pairs, learners take it in turns to say the words. Play the tape again for them to check their pronunciation.

7 In production

7A Processes

Action

- **Read about production processes**
- **Listen to a description of a production process**
- **Describe a production process**
- **Grammar: present perfect passive**

Reading and Speaking: production processes

1 Find out if learners have ever made any sweets or chocolates. Encourage them to describe how they made them. Learners then discuss the exercise in pairs or as a class.

2 If possible, bring in a chocolate which has a filling and covering. Learners discuss how they think it is made: check learners understand *pour*. They read the article and summarise the enrobing process. Check answers.

3 **a** Learners read the text and decide the order of the pictures. Check answers: elicit the number of the first picture (*F*) and get learners to read out the relevant part of the text. Check any new vocabulary.
b Elicit which verb forms are used in the two texts. Discuss the reasons as a class.

Key

2 The centre is made first, and then liquid chocolate is poured over it.
3a F, I, G, D, C, A, B, H, E
b The second text includes passive rather than active verb forms. This is usual for a more formal (or written) description of a process. Passive verb forms are also used because the person doing each action is obvious or unimportant.

Grammar: present perfect passive

4 Refer learners back to the text in Exercise 3. Elicit three examples of the present perfect passive. Write a complete sentence on the board, e.g. *After the squares have been cooled, they are taken off the conveyor and put in trays.* Discuss the exercise in pairs or as a class. Use the board to highlight answers. If necessary, establish how the present simple passive is formed.

5 Learners rewrite the sentences using passive verb forms. Check answers.

Key

4 Examples: have been cooled; have been folded; have been passed
a *has / have + been + past participle*
b To emphasise that an action takes place before another one.

5a Liquid chocolate is brought into the factory in lorries.
b After the filling has been made, it is taken to the cool room.
c The nuts are imported from the US.
d These have been decorated, and now they are sent through the cooling tunnel.
e The factory kitchen is kept clean.

Extra practice

P 7.1 Check learners know *pizza bases* and *olives*. Learners work in pairs. Photocopy the worksheet on page 80 for **A** and **B**. Give Learner **A** the cut up pictures. Learner **A** decides which is the first stage and describes it to **B**, e.g. *First you place the pizza bases on the tray.* **B** completes the text using the passive form. At the end of the activity, they check the text and complete the final stage of the process.

Key

a are placed   **b** is made   **c** has been poured
d are decorated   **e** are cut   **f** have been weighed
g are packed   **h** are delivered   **i** are cooked

Speaking and Listening: describing a production process

6 **a** Check learners know *shell* and *mould*. Learners discuss the process in pairs and as a class. Do not confirm their answers yet.
b Learners listen to the tape and make notes about the process. Check answers.
c Discuss as a class.
d Check learners know how to use the words in the box. In pairs, learners use their notes from **b** and the sequence words to describe the process.

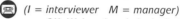 *(I = interviewer   M = manager)*

I: *OK. We've already looked at one production process, where you make the centre first and then cover it with chocolate. I can see how that works when the fillings are quite hard, but what about chocolates with soft centres?*

M: *Yes, that's right. Of course, we can't use the same process with chocolates that have very soft centres – the soft creams and the liqueurs. For these we use what we call the moulding process.*

I: *So what happens in the moulding process? How is it different?*

M: *Well, the main difference is that we make the chocolate shells first. After they've been made, we pour the filling into them. The first thing that happens is that liquid chocolate is poured into a tray of moulds. Then the tray is turned over quickly – in this way the extra chocolate falls out and leaves a very thin layer on the sides and bottom of each mould.*

I: *Ah . . . I see; that's how you do it!*

M: *Yes, it's simple really. Then the moulds are cooled – to make the shells hard – and then we pour in the cream fillings. After the filling has been put in, they go into the cooling tunnel for a second time and then a thin layer of chocolate is put on top of the cream. Finally, after cooling again we take the finished chocolates out of the moulds and pack them by hand.*

7 If you wish, ask learners to think of a process before the lesson. They can describe their process in small groups. Alternatively, with a small group, learners can give a presentation. Encourage them to draw simple pictures to illustrate the process.

Key

6c In the *moulding process*, the chocolate shell is made first. In the *enrobing process*, the centres are made first.

d suggested answer
First, the chocolate shells are made. After the liquid chocolate has been poured into the tray of moulds, the tray is turned over quickly, leaving a thin layer of chocolate in each mould. When the moulds have been cooled, the cream filling is poured in, and a thin layer of chocolate is put on top. The chocolates are cooled again, and then they are packed by hand.

7B The right approach

Action

- **Listen to and describe qualities for a job**
- **Vocabulary: factory jobs, personal qualities and skills**
- **Grammar: adverbs**

Vocabulary: factory jobs

Learners discuss these questions in small groups or as a class.

- **Have you visited or worked in a factory? What was it like?**
- **What are the advantages and disadvantages of working in a factory?**
- **What jobs do people do in a factory?**

1 In pairs, learners look at the photographs and discuss the exercise. Check answers. See if the jobs are the same as the ones they discussed.

Key

1a A in a factory; checking quality
B in a factory; operating a machine
C in a factory; assembling a car
D in a factory; packing goods
E in a factory; assessing production
b A quality control manager   B machine operator
C assembler   D packer   E production manager

Listening: qualities for a job

2 Copy the exercise onto the board. Play the tape for the learners to complete the sentences. Check answers. Complete the sentences on the board. Establish the difference between *must* and *should*. Highlight what follows *should be able to / have / be*. Leave the sentences there for Exercise 4.

🔊 *Packing is an important part of the production process because it's the packaging that a customer sees first. A good packer in a factory should be able to work quickly and carefully. He or she should be good with their hands . . . and in some packing jobs they need to write labels, so a packer should have clear handwriting.*

Key

2 A good packer should be able to work quickly and carefully.
A good packer should be good with their hands.
A good packer should have clear handwriting.

Vocabulary: personal qualities and skills

3 Check learners understand the headings in the exercise. Then direct them to the phrases in Exercise 4. Demonstrate the task: ask *Which words or phrases are about money?* Establish that some of the qualities may go under more than one heading. In pairs, learners do the same with the other headings. Check answers, drilling for correct pronunciation as necessary.

4 Refer learners back to the photographs in Exercise 1 and the sentences on the board from Exercise 2. Ask a learner to read out the example. In pairs, learners discuss the jobs in the same way. Encourage them to make notes: they will need these for Exercise 7. Discuss their ideas as a class.

Key

3a financial skills; good with figures
b good timekeeping; punctual; a fast worker; work fast
c planning skills; plan carefully
d good communication skills; calm; reliable; patient; work as part of a team
e planning skills; good communication skills; a good leader; solve problems calmly; work well as part of a team; make decisions quickly
f technical understanding; an interest in science
g a desire to do a good job; strong and fit; neat; clean; do repetitive tasks accurately; concentrate easily; work hard; work independently

4 suggested answers
I think a packer should be a fast worker.
I think a machine operator should have technical understanding.
I think a production manager should be able to solve problems calmly.
I think an assembler should be able to do repetitive tasks accurately.

Grammar: adverbs

5 Copy the two phrases onto the board. Establish what part of speech *good* and *carefully* are. Learners discuss **a** and **b**. Books closed. Copy the table in **c** onto the board. In pairs, learners complete the table with the adverbs. Books open. They look at the last column in Exercise 4 and check their answers. Discuss how regular adverbs are formed.

6 Learners complete the sentences for themselves. If you wish, they can mingle, read out their sentences and find out how many learners have written the same.

Key

5a how someone should plan
b verbs
c carefully, calmly, accurately, independently, quickly, easily, well, fast, hard
By adding *ly* to the adjective. If the adjective ends in *y*, this changes to *i*.
6 **suggested answers**
a calmly **b** well **c** carefully **d** fast **e** clearly

Speaking: describing qualities for a job

7 Learners work in pairs. Refer them back to the notes they made in Exercise 4. Using their notes, they do the exercise.

8 Learners discuss the exercise in pairs and as a class.

Extra practice

As an extension, learners work in small groups. They think of a different (if possible, unusual) job and write six sentences using the language in Exercises 2 and 4. The first group reads out their first sentence: the others try to guess the job. If they do, they get six points. If they don't, the first group reads out the next sentence. If the others guess the job, they get five points. If they don't, the first group continues in the same way. If no one guesses their job, they get six points.

7C Product specifications

Action

- Discuss job responsibilities
- Read about a job
- Listen to a description of a product sheet
- Read and write faxes and accompanying letters
- Vocabulary: phrases of purpose, reason and result

Speaking: job responsibilities

1 Use the picture to check learners understand *carton* and *pallet*. Also check *shelf-life*. Direct them to the people in the exercise. Demonstrate the task: ask *Who is interested in the number and types of chocolates in a ballotin of Neuhaus chocolates?* Elicit their ideas. In pairs, learners do the same with the other specifications. Copy the specifications onto the board. As you discuss their ideas as a class, note down the people (a, b, etc.). Leave them there for the next exercise.

Key

1 • the number and type of chocolates: a b c d e
• the weight of the chocolates: a b d e
• the weight of the packaging: d
• the type of packaging: a d e
• the shelf-life of the chocolates: a c d e
• the number of ballotins in a carton: c d
• the number of cartons on a pallet: c
• the alcohol content: a b
• the price: a b d e

Reading about a job

2 Learners read the text to check their ideas from Exercise 1. Tick ✓ which guesses were correct on the board. Discuss **b** as a class.

Key

2a • a customer in a shop: the alcohol content
• a customs officer: the alcohol content
• a storeman: the number of ballotins in a carton, the number of cartons on a pallet
• a manager of a shop in the US: the number and type of chocolates, the shelf-life of the chocolates
• a marketing manager of a hotel: the number and type of chocolates, the shelf-life of the chocolates
b It should give detailed information about the product, which allows a retailer to assemble the product correctly and consistently.

Vocabulary: phrases of reason, purpose and result

3 Copy the three sentences onto the board.
• **The purpose of these** + <u>is</u> + <u>to give</u> detailed information ...
• **The reason why** + <u>this is important</u> + is <u>that</u> alcohol ....
• **The result is** + <u>that</u> retailers can ...

Learners discuss the exercise. Highlight the answers on the board.

4 Learners complete the sentences about themselves. They compare answers in small groups and as a class.

Key

3b the purpose: to give detailed information . . .
the reason: that alcohol can't be imported . . .
the result: that retailers can assemble . . .
4 **suggested answers**
a The reason why I live in my town is that I found a job here.
b The result of working hard is that you are given more work.
c The purpose of studying English is to find a better-paid job.

Extra practice

P 7.2 Learners work in small groups. Make a photocopy of the worksheet on page 81. Learners complete the sentences. In pairs, each learner reads out the first part of a sentence in a random order to see if their partner can guess the second half.

Key

suggested answers
a The result of being rude to your boss . . .
b The result of driving too fast . . .
c The purpose of having an answer machine . . .
d The purpose of going on holiday . . .
e The reason why I don't work in the evenings . . .
f The reason why he applied for a new job . . .

Listening to a description of a product sheet

5 Learners listen to Sylvia and complete the chart. Check answers.

 I'll give you an example of a product sheet. Here's the one on the mini ballotin that we sell a lot of to airlines. It tells you the number of chocolates, which in the mini ballotin is two. Then there's the total weight . . . 33 grams . . . that's with the ballotin . . . and the weight without the ballotin . . . 28 grams. Then the ballotins are packed inside a larger carton for transportation. When you look at this sheet it shows you that each carton holds 84 mini ballotins. Oh, and the shelf-life – everyone needs to know about that. For these chocolates it's four months. For some of our other ones, with fresh cream, it's one month.

Key

5	Product	Mini Ballotin	Total weight	**33 grams**
	No. of chocolates	**2**	Shelf-life	**4 months**
	Weight of chocolates	**28 grams**	No. of mini ballotins in a carton	**84**

Reading and writing faxes and accompanying letters

6 Learners read the letter and fax to answer the questions.

7 Elicit the layout of a fax and write it on the board. If appropriate, compare it with the layout that the learners use at work. Each learner writes a fax to Sylvia using the information in the exercise. Then they swap faxes with their partner and write the reply.

Key

6a Saudi Arabia   **b** a product sheet for the mini ballotin

Grammar backup 7

The passive: present perfect passive

Key

1b are mixed, are added   **c** has been seasoned, is rolled
d is placed   **e** has been reached, are grilled
f are served
2b has already been booked.
 c has been checked, it is sent to their customers.
 d the bills always paid by the accounts department?
 e have been lost by the bank.
 f have been broken by the new cleaner.

Adverbs

Key

1b late   **c** hard   **d** well   **e** slowly   **f** lately   **g** good
2b fast   **c** good cook   **d** slowly   **e** very quietly / softly
3   **suggested answers**
 a well   **b** good   **c** early   **d** motivated

8 Exporting

8A Dealing with export queries

Action

- Listen to an interview
- Describe tasks
- Listen to a job description
- Describe continuing change
- Write a fax
- Vocabulary: exporting
- Grammar: *have* something *done*

Vocabulary: exporting

1 Check learners understand *to export*. Discuss what their country exports and imports. Copy the headings onto the board. Demonstrate the task: elicit that *deliver* goes under the heading *To send* and write it on the board. In pairs, learners categorise the words in the same way. Check answers and drill for correct pronunciation. Establish that *despatch* and *enquiry* can be also spelt *dispatch* and *inquiry*.

Key

1 • To send: deliver, despatch, transport, ship
   • To communicate: contact, fax, speak to, discuss
   • A customer: client, buyer
   • A question: query, problem, inquiry

Speaking and Listening: a job description

2 Learners discuss the exercise in pairs.

3 Learners listen to the tape and tick ✓ the tasks that Karin mentions. Compare what she says with their ideas from Exercise 2.

Well ... everything that concerns exports from handling questions from clients to contact with new clients to ... er ... making sure that the orders are passed on to the despatch department, to the invoicing department ... um ... handling everything concerning transport, contacting transport companies ... er ... sending out client information about the flight details for everything ... so everything from A to Z.

USA, UK ... um ... Japan, but I'm not dealing with Japan at the moment, that's someone else. Who else? We have a lot of clients in ... um ... in Europe, most of our clients are in Europe ... and we are more and more selling towards the Middle East and the Far East. That's working better and better now.

4 Learners listen to the tape and answer the questions. Check answers.

Key

3 a, b, c, f, g
4a the United States, the UK, Europe, the Middle East, the Far East
 b absolutely everything (the whole range of tasks)
 c *Better and better* emphasises the continuous nature of the improvement over a period of time.

Speaking: describing continuing change

5 a Copy this onto the board:
   more and more
   higher and higher
   less and less important
   more and more difficult
   better and better

Refer learners to the Phrasebook. Elicit the opposite of *more and more* and write **less and less** on the board. Learners do the same with the other expressions. Check answers. If necessary, refer them back to Grammar backup 5 for rules on the formation of comparative adjectives.
b Learners complete the sentences. Compare answers in small groups and as a class. Brainstorm other examples, e.g. *hotter and hotter, less and less patient*. If you wish, learners can find adjectives in earlier wordlists: in pairs, they make sentences to read out to the class.

Key

5a • We're selling less and less.
   • Costs are getting lower and lower.
   • North Africa is becoming more and more important.
   • Finding good staff is less and less difficult / easier and easier.
 b **suggested answers**
   • I'm working harder and harder every year.
   • The price of oil is getting higher and higher each year.
   • My English is getting better and better.
   • The market for luxury chocolates is getting more and more competitive.
   • The dollar is becoming stronger and stronger against our currency.

Grammar: *have* something *done*

6 Learners read the fax extract and answer the questions. Check answers. For **d**, write **I will have a sample pack sent to you** on the board. Highlight the *have* something *done* construction. Build up a table on the board with different verb forms, e.g. past simple, going to etc.

7 Learners do the exercise. Check answers. Do the exercises in the Grammar backup for more practice.

8 Write these headings on the board:

us	someone else

Use the picture to set up the situation. If you wish, brainstorm the kinds of things you need when you start a business, e.g. furniture, phone lines etc. In pairs, learners discuss what they're going to do and what they are going to have done. Make sure they complete their plan. Compare plans as a class. Decide which pair will need the least money to set up their company.

Key

6a Someone in the export or sales department of a company, like Karin Thielemans.

b A new possible customer.

c Send the documentation by courier. Speak to the Production Department.

d Send a sample pack by air. We know that someone else is going to do it because the fax says 'have a sample pack sent'.

e suggested answer

Dear _____

I am a buyer for a large supermarket group in Greece, and we are interested in your products.

Could you please send me information about your full product range, with price lists. We would also like to see any sample products that are available.

I look forward to hearing from you.

Yours faithfully

7b They're having new brochures printed.

c They're going to have a new house built.

d The company will have some heaters installed.

e We're having / going to have the machines repaired.

f She has had her car cleaned.

8 suggested answers

We'll have the room painted.

We'll have the carpet cleaned.

We'll have some new furniture delivered.

We'll put some pictures on the walls.

We'll have two phone lines installed.

We'll have a new logo designed.

We'll advertise for a secretary.

We'll employ a receptionist.

We'll have a new brochure written.

Writing a fax

9 Learners read the fax. Elicit which things they are going to do personally. Remind them of the words in Exercise 1. They write the reply fax and then compare faxes in pairs. For feedback, elicit a model fax, line by line, and write it on the board. Learners correct any errors in their own writing.

Key

9 suggested answer

Thank you for your fax requesting information about our products.

I am sending you our catalogue and current price list of export products by courier today. I will speak to the finance and production departments and have a company report and sample products despatched to you as soon as possible.

Our sales manager, Tony Doyle, will contact you directly to arrange a visit.

Yours sincerely

8B Franchise businesses

Action

- Read about franchises
- Make hypothetical statements
- Vocabulary: franchise businesses, nouns ending in -ee/-er
- Grammar: second conditional sentences

Speaking and Reading: franchises

1 Find out if learners have heard of Jeff de Bruges. In pairs, learners look at the pictures and discuss the questions. Compare answers as a class but do not confirm them yet.

Key

1a A franchise is permission (usually exclusive) to sell a company's products or services in a particular area.

b • All the shops look exactly the same.

• The products that they sell are identical.

• All stock is bought from the parent company.

c suggested answers

McDonald's (hamburgers), Pizza Hut (pizzas)

d *buyer:* advantages – established name and products; exclusive geographical area; existing design of shop and packaging; provision of staff training; provision of products; national and international advertising and promotion; general support from the parent company

disadvantages – high setting-up costs; obligation to buy and sell only the products of the parent company; percentage of profits paid to parent company; risk of losing franchise

parent company: advantages – income from licence; regular income from shop sales; guaranteed sales of products; retailer takes the risk; control over brand reputation

disadvantages – some dependence on performance of franchisee for sale of company products

Reading about franchise businesses

2 Learners read the text to compare their answers from Exercise 1. Check answers.

3 Write **a–i** on the board. Get learners to find *reputation* in the text. Decide which definition it is and write **reputation** next to **f**. Learners do the same with the other words. Compare answers in pairs. Write them on the board, mark the stress and drill for correct pronunciation.

Key

3a network **b** share **c** licence **d** exclusive **e** fittings **f** reputation **g** damage **h** personnel **i** support

Vocabulary: nouns ending in -ee/-er

4 Learners read out the sentence from the text with *franchisee*. Discuss the exercise in pairs or as a class. Establish that the main stress falls on the *-ee* suffix.

4a The company that buys the right to run the shop.
 b • The person who performs the action ends in *-er:*
   trainer, interviewer, employer.
  • The person who the action is done to ends in *-ee:*
   trainee, interviewee, employee.
 c addressee: someone who a letter is addressed to
  licensee: someone who a licence is given to
  payee: someone who receives money

Grammar: second conditional sentences

5 Copy the two sentences onto the board. Ask learners to find them in the text. Discuss the exercise. Use the board to highlight answers.

6 Learners read the example situation. Establish why the sentence uses the second, not first, conditional. In pairs, learners write sentences for each situation: make sure they follow the pattern *if* + prompt + effect. They read out their sentences as a class. Decide which one is the most realistic.

7 Learners complete the sentences about themselves. Compare answers in small groups and as a class.

Key

5a A is more likely than B.
 b A – present simple, B – past simple
 c A – *will* + infinitive, B – *would* + infinitive
  we'll = we will / shall, we'd = we would
 d When a situation is possible but unlikely. *If* clause with past simple, clause with *would* + infinitive.
6 **suggested answers**
 a If we increase the prices of products slightly, sales probably won't fall much.
 b If we doubled staff salaries, we'd go out of business.
 c If we send the parcel by sea, it'll be there in three weeks.
 d If we let the staff go on holiday at the same time, the factory would have to close.
 e If we didn't receive a share of the profits from a franchisee, we would take that franchisee to court.

8C Assisting callers

Action

- ■ Describe a receptionist's duties
- ■ Receive a visitor
- ■ Understand and take messages
- ■ Say no politely
- ■ Vocabulary: reception duties

Speaking: reception duties

1 Learners look at the photograph of Eliane and the verbs and nouns. In pairs, they list things that she does in her job. Discuss as a class.

Key

1 **suggested answers**
 She welcomes visitors, makes appointments, takes messages, sends faxes, helps visitors, receives courier packages, puts through telephone calls, arranges meetings, gives directions, keeps a diary.

Listening and Speaking: receiving a visitor

2 Learners listen to the conversation and answer the questions. Check answers.

(V = visitor   E = Eliane)
 v: *Hello.*
 E: *Good morning. Can I help you?*
 v: *Er ... I've got an appointment with Karin Thielemans ... at 11.30. I'm a little early.*
 E: *I see. Could I take your name?*
 v: *Yes. It's Alan Walker.*
 E: *And which company are you from, Mr Walker?*
 v: *Sweetman Limited.*
 E: *Sweetman?*
 v: *Yes, that's right.*
 E: *Right. Just a moment, please. I'll call her. (Hello. It's Eliane. I have Mr Walker to see you from Sweetman Limited ... Yes, OK.) She'll be down in a few minutes, Mr Walker. Would you like to take a seat?*
 v: *Thank you very much.*
 E: *Excuse me ...*

3 Play the tape again for the learners to complete the conversation. Check answers. Learners practise the conversation in pairs.

4 Copy these sentences onto the board.
 • ...... you ...... me your name?
 • ...... you ... me the ...... of your company, please?
 • ...... a moment. I ...... her you're here.
 • ...... I ...... you something to drink?
 • ...... I ...... your coat?

In pairs, learners complete the sentences. Then they check their answers with the Phrasebook. Drill for correct stress and rhythm as necessary.

Divide learners into pairs. They read the information and roleplay their conversations. Make sure they change roles. Note down any errors you hear. For feedback, two pairs work together. The first pair roleplays their conversation: the other pair corrects any errors they hear. Then they change over. Finally use the board to correct any errors.

Key

2a Karin Thielemans **b** 11.30 **c** C
3 See tapescript.

Listening and Reading: telephone messages

5 First learners read the three messages. Then they listen to the phone calls and match them with the messages. Check answers.

1 (R = receptionist   C = caller)

R: *Good morning. Blane International. Can I help you?*

C: *Oh, hello. Er ... Is Jennifer Street there, please?*

R: *I'm afraid she's just gone out. She'll be back this afternoon, though.*

C: *Ah ...*

R: *Would you like to leave her a message?*

C: *Er ... well ... yes, I think so.*

R: *OK. Just a moment. Right. What message would you like to leave?*

C: *Can you ask her to meet me after work ... at six o'clock ... er ... in the cafe across the road ... er ... you know ...*

R: *The Opera Cafe?*

C: *Yes, that's it, the Opera Cafe.*

R: *OK. And can I take your name?*

C: *Oh yes. It's John Locker.*

R: *John Locker ...*

2 (R = receptionist   C = caller)

R: *Hello. Blane International. Can I help you?*

C: *Yes. My name's Helen Beard, and I've got a meeting with Tom Williams this afternoon at four ...*

R: *Yes ...*

C: *And I'm calling to cancel it because I'm afraid I'm ill.*

R: *Ah, right. I'll pass that on to him. Can I just have your name again, please?*

C: *Helen Beard. My number's 652418.*

R: *Beard. And your meeting was at four o'clock this afternoon?*

C: *That's right.*

R: *Don't worry. I'll let him know.*

C: *Thanks. Oh, there's one other thing.*

R: *Yes?*

C: *Can you tell him I'll put the report in the post. He should get it tomorrow morning.*

R: *Yes, of course. Thank you for calling.*

3 (R = receptionist   C = caller)

R: *Good morning. Blane International. How can I help you?*

C: *Oh, hello Tim, this is Kate ... Kate Allen.*

R: *Hello Mrs Allen. How are you?*

C: *Oh, fine thanks. Look, is Peter there?*

R: *No, I'm afraid he's out at the moment.*

C: *Oh ... well ... can you ask him to call me? I'm going out right now but I'll be back about two. Could you ask him to call me as soon as possible after that?*

R: *Certainly, after two o'clock.*

C: *That's right. See you soon then.*

6 Play the messages again for learners to note down the missing information. Check answers.

Key

5 1 C   2 A   3 B

6 A She's cancelled the meeting with you at four o'clock this afternoon because she's ill.

B ... as soon as possible after two o'clock.

C ... at six o'clock in the Opera Cafe.

Speaking: saying *no* politely

7 Learners discuss the exercise in pairs and as a class.

8 Demonstrate the task: ask *Can I see Ms Thielemans?* Elicit a polite reply. In pairs, learners make up similar exchanges for each situation. For feedback, volunteer pairs roleplay their exchanges. Decide if the 'receptionists' are polite.

Key

7 Because a reason is given and the speaker expresses regret (*I'm afraid ...*).

8 **suggested answers**

a I'm afraid she's not here at the moment. She's abroad on business.

b I'm afraid you've come to the wrong building. You want the one opposite.

c I'm afraid the company has a no-smoking policy. Shall I show you the roof garden?

d I'm afraid the shop's closed until tomorrow. It always closes at five.

e I'm afraid we're not allowed to make personal calls from the office. The telephone bills are getting too high.

Extra practice

P 8.1 This activity revises some of the vocabulary from the unit and the conditionals. Make one photocopy of the worksheet on page 81 per six students. Learners work in pairs. Divide the words so that each pair has at least six words. The aim of the activity is to collect sets of words that are related. Each set must have a minimum of three words. First the pairs decide which words they are going to collect and which they are going to give away. Then they mingle, tell the other learners what words they do not want and try to bargain for the words they want to collect, e.g. *I'll give you despatch if you give me query*. The pair with the most logical sets of words wins.

Grammar backup 8

Have something *done*

Key

1b She had her suit cleaned yesterday.

c They have just had the photocopier repaired.

d I have the tyres checked every six months.

e Did you have the book cover designed last week?

f We are having our office redecorated at the moment.

Second conditional

Key

1a 3   **b** 1   **c** 6   **d** 2   **e** 4   **f** 5

3b If it **doesn't** rain this afternoon, I'll go for a walk.

c She would get the job if she **spoke** better English.

d If they **invite** me, I'll go with them.

e They'd get more work done if they **were** more efficient.

g If I were you, I'd / **would** fly first class.

h What **would** you do if you won a lot of money?

9A Viewing

Action

- Read the results of a survey
- Discuss programme types
- Understand and describe preferences
- Read and write a viewer profile
- Vocabulary: programme types, compounds with *well-* and *badly-*

Vocabulary: programme types

To introduce the topic, write these questions on the board:
- **How many TV channels do you have at home?**
- **How many hours of TV do you usually watch a day?**
- **What was the last programme you watched? Why?**

Learners discuss them in small groups or as a class. Compare the last programmes they watched with the results in the survey to see if they like the same kinds of programmes.

1 a and b Learners do the exercises in pairs. Check as a class. To extend their vocabulary, draw this mindmap on the board:

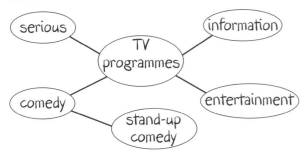

As a class, decide where to put the TV programmes in **a** and **b**. In pairs, learners then brainstorm other kinds of programmes they know. Write their answers on the board. Drill for correct pronunciation. Leave them there for Exercise 3.

c Demonstrate the task with academy awards, e.g. the Brit awards in the UK for pop music. In pairs, learners give other examples of programmes in their country. If you wish, include the programmes on the mindmap. For feedback, learners say the programme to see if the others know what type it is.

Key

1a • Academy awards • stand-up comedy • music
   • variety shows • game shows • news • sitcoms
b cartoon, talk show, music show

Listening and Speaking: describing preferences

2 Learners listen to the tape and complete the chart. Check answers.

 A: Oh ... I can't stand game shows. I prefer watching concerts and music videos. They're much better.
B: I don't watch any sports programmes ... and there's so much sport on! My favourite programmes are movies – you know, Hollywood films. They're the best.
C: I enjoy comedy programmes, but I prefer the live stand-up shows to sitcoms. Most of those sitcoms are really stupid – especially the American ones.
D: Soap operas always make me turn off. But I watch cartoons a lot.
E: I'm interested in some sports, but I like football better than athletics. And those other ones they call sport ... you know, snooker ... and darts ... I can't stand them. But the worst programmes for me are the talk shows. They're so boring!

3 Copy these sentences onto the board:
a I .... game shows.
b I .... concerts.
c My ...... programmes are movies.
d They're ....
e I ...... comedy programmes.
f I ...... the live stand-up shows ...... sitcoms.
g I'...... .... some sports.
h I ...... football .... athletics.

Play the tape again. Learners complete the sentences. Check as a class on the board. Drill the sentences for correct stress and intonation. Learners look at the Phrasebook and identify the ones which aren't on the board. Then they use the expressions and the mindmap to discuss their viewing preferences. Make sure they give reasons. Compare preferences as a class.

Key

2	Likes	Dislikes
	A concerts, music / videos	game shows
	B movies	sports programmes
	C live stand-up shows	sitcoms
	D cartoons	soap operas
	E football	snooker, darts, talk shows

Extra practice

Learners work in small groups. Each group has a photocopy of today's television viewing schedule, e.g. from a newspaper. Together they plan what they are going to watch. Make sure they write their schedule down. Then they report what their decision is to the class, giving reasons, e.g. *At 7 o'clock, we're going to watch a nature programme on tigers because Luis is very interested in them.*

Reading: a viewer profile

4 a Learners discuss the questions in pairs or as a class.
b Check learners understand *brand*, *trendsetters* and *whizz-kids*. They read the text and make notes under the two headings. Check answers.
c Learners discuss the exercise in pairs and as a class.

d Copy this chart onto the board:

positive	negative

In pairs, learners categorise the adjectives. Write their answers on the board, mark the stress and drill for correct pronunciation. Say the definitions below and elicit the adjectives in brackets to check understanding:
- *The opposite of stupid is ... .* (intelligent)
- *If you have a good education in different subjects, you are ... .* (well-educated)
- *If you spend time thinking about things or people, you are ... .* (thoughtful)
- *People who are willing to consider new ideas are ... .* (open-minded)

In pairs, learners then use the adjectives to describe a typical MTV viewer. Compare ideas as a class. Find out which channels they watch and what kind of viewer they are.

Key

4a The company can then make or broadcast programmes that its audience will enjoy. It hopes to increase viewing figures and therefore to sell more advertising.
b What MTV viewers do: make key purchase decisions; love shopping, buying brands; buy all the latest technology.
What MTV viewers are: decision makers; ultra consumers; trendsetters; style leaders; arbiters of taste; electronics whizz-kids; opinion leaders; well-read on all the key issues; well-travelled; multi-lingual; high achievers; well-educated; world citizens.
c suggested answers
Internet software because they buy all the latest technology; travel books because they are well-travelled; fashion magazines because they are style leaders.
d suggested answers
Modern because they are trendsetters and style leaders; independent because they are decision makers; open-minded because they are well-read and well-educated.

Vocabulary: compounds with *well- / badly-*

5 a Elicit examples of compound words with *well-* from the text and write them on the board. Discuss **a**. Establish the difference in meaning between *well-read* for a person, i.e. someone who has read of lot of different literature, and *well-read* for a book, i.e. a copy of a book which has been read by a lot of people.
b Ask two learners to read out the example sentences. Learners rewrite the sentences in the same way. Check answers.

Key

5a a past participle
b • The reception was badly-planned.
• This letter is badly-written.
• He is well-dressed.
• The product was badly-promoted.

Speaking and Writing: a viewer profile

6 With the learners, list different TV stations on the board. In pairs, they choose one station and write a viewer profile. Compare profiles as a class. If you wish, they can display them for the other learners to read.

9B MTV Europe

Action
- **Talk and read about a company**
- **Listen for main points**
- **Rephrasing**
- **Read and write slogans**

Speaking and reading about a company

1 Establish whether learners know / watch MTV. Learners discuss the exercise in pairs or as a class.

2a and b Direct learners to the photographs and text on page 72. Learners discuss the questions in pairs.
c–e They read the text and look at the photograph to answer the questions. Check answers.

Key

2a The product of a particular company, which is sold all over the world.
c About 1064 million. A household is the people who live in a single house.
d • Geographical areas, each made up of one or more countries.
• Television stations that are linked to MTV and broadcast its programmes.

Listening for main points

3 In pairs, learners decide if they think the statements are true or false. Compare ideas but do not confirm answers yet. Play the tape for them to compare their ideas and to correct the false statements. Check answers.

(I = interviewer   R = Iain Renwick)
I: *One of the slogans that MTV uses describes an important part of their philosophy. The slogan is, 'Think globally, act locally'. MTV is clearly global – you can watch its programmes all over the world, but how does it try to provide for local needs? What about the language of the programmes, for example?*
R: *The practical reality is that the international language of music is predominantly English. But in saying that the reflection in our programming content and the content of the channels across the world is driven by the needs of the local markets. So we do have – in Brazil for instance we have a completely Portuguese service. It's language specific. So in south-east Asia we're going language specific – we've got a Mandarin service, we've got an English language service, we've got a Hindi service, we're seeing that developing more in Europe.*
I: *And what about content? Is the content of MTV programmes the same all over the world?*

R: *There's obviously a lot of programming that's produced that covers all our channels, and that will be predominantly having been developed in English. So there'll be programming delivered from the European market, from North America that goes into our affiliates throughout the world. But that would be mainly reflected in major award shows – the video music awards in New York, the MTV Europe music awards, the movie awards in LA which MTV does. So there'll always be ... MTV is a global ... it thinks internationally but it can deliver relevance to its local audiences by understanding their preferences but presenting them with the big picture as well, and that's very very important.*
One cannot deliver solely with one message for Europe; one has to still clearly, clearly, clearly recognise the cultural diversity and that is to us a huge strength of Europe, is that cultural diversity and that's something that MTV is reflecting in its structure, in its growing regional structure, in its ability to say yes, we will speak pan-nationally but we'll clearly understand your, your ... specific requirements, whether it's in Germany, whether it's in Italy, whether it's in the U.K.

Key

3a False. There are programmes in Portuguese, Mandarin and Hindi.
b False. Many of the programmes are produced for local markets.

Reading and Speaking: rephrasing

4 Write the example sentence on the board and discuss how it can be written with simpler language. Write the new version on the board. Learners do the same for the other sentences. Compare answers in pairs. Then write the simplest versions on the board.

5 Write **In other words** on the board. Read out the example sentence and get the learners to rephrase it beginning with *In other words*. Write other expressions learners know like **In other words** on the board. Direct them to the Phrasebook to see if they are the same. In pairs, learners use the expressions to practise rephrasing the sentences in Exercise 4. Check answers as a class.

6 Check learners understand *plot*. Demonstrate the task with a film you have seen: as you describe the plot, be deliberately unclear so that the learners have to ask you to rephrase. Then give them time to think about a film plot. In pairs, they take it in turns to tell each other the plot. Monitor and note down any errors you hear. Correct them at the end of the activity.

Key

4a Programmes are made to meet local needs.
b More and more programmes in south-east Asia are in local languages.
c Many of the programmes are shown in every country.
d We must produce programmes that reflect cultural differences around Europe.

Reading and Writing: slogans

7 a and b Remind learners of the MTV slogan. Discuss if they think it is appropriate. Discuss the questions in pairs or as a class.
c If possible, bring in some newspaper / magazine advertisements to prompt the learners. Discuss as a class.
d Learners discuss their slogans in small groups. They compare them as a class and decide which one is the best. If they need help in choosing a product, bring in advertisements with the slogans cut out. When they have written theirs, they compare it with the original slogan.

Key

7 • Be yourself. The product helps you to be yourself as an individual.
• Some cars (Honda cars) are better than other cars.
• The sound systems are so attractive to look at and produce sounds of such high quality that you can feel the music as well as hear it.

Extra practice

If you have access to video, record some TV advertisements. The first time, show them with the sound down. Discuss what they are advertising and what images they remember. If the advertisements have slogans, see if the learners know them. Play the adverts again with the sound up. Check answers and discuss why they are effective.

9C Special events

Action

- **Talk about events**
- **Read and write a letter**
- **Vocabulary: reporting verbs**
- **Grammar: reported speech**

Speaking: special events

1 Learners look at the pictures and discuss the questions.

Key

1a musicians   **b** an awards ceremony
suggested answers
d Oscars are presented to actors and film makers at an annual award ceremony.
e Congratulations.
f Thank you. It's a great honour.

Grammar: reported speech

2 a Copy the example sentence onto the board. Elicit the reporting verb and underline it. Learners do the same with the other sentences. Check answers.
b Elicit other reporting verbs the learners know. Write them on the board.

3 a–d Learners discuss the exercise in pairs and as a class.
e Copy the chart onto the board. Learners complete it. Check answers. Establish that *would (like)* does not change.

> ### Key
> **2a** • said • asked • replied • added • asked • explained • told, said
> **3a** • statements: said, replied, added, explained, told
> • questions: asked
> **b** tell
> **c** • The presenter announced that the company was giving a special award.
> • The singer replied that they had just finished one.
> • The presenter asked if they enjoyed touring.
> **d** • 'The award is for the best new band.'
> • When will the band make their next new album?
> • The band are going to tour Europe in the summer.
> • We would like to tour as much as possible.
> • We are honoured to receive the award but we cannot accept it.
> **e**
>
> | direct speech | reported speech |
> |---|---|
> | **is giving** | was giving |
> | **is** | was |
> | **will make** | would make |
> | **have just finished** | had just finished |
> | **are going to tour** | were going to tour |
> | **enjoy** | enjoyed |
> | **would like to tour** | would like to tour |
> | **are honoured** | were honoured |
> | **cannot accept** | could not accept |

Extra practice

P 9.1 Photocopy the messages on page 82. Learners work in threes and take it in turns to report the answer machine messages. Learner **A** reads out their message; **B** reports it to **C**; **C** writes it down. Then they swap roles. Finally they compare the answer machine messages with their reported versions.

Reading and Writing: a letter

4 Learners read the letter. If necessary, use these questions to check the details: *What time are they arriving? How many rooms do they need? What kind of food do they want? What kind of transport do they want? How are they going to pay?* In pairs, learners look at the pictures and discuss the problems the band had at the hotel. Check answers.

5 Establish that learners will need to use the language in Exercises 2 and 3. They write the letter in pairs. For feedback, they exchange their letters with another pair to check for errors.

> ### Key
> **4** When they arrived, their rooms weren't ready. They had single beds, not double ones. They needed a minibus but were given a car. They are vegetarians but were given chicken to eat. They were asked to pay the bill themselves, but it wasn't their responsibility.

5 suggested answer
Dear Mr Edmunds
I am writing to complain about the service the *Motel Lizards* received at your hotel last night.
When we discussed arrangements on the phone, I explained that the band would arrive at 11 a.m. They arrived at that time, but the rooms were not ready for them. I also asked you for five double rooms, but they were shown to single rooms. I explained that the band needed a minibus, but they were offered a normal-sized car. I told you all the band members were vegetarian, but you prepared meat for them. And finally, I asked you if you would send the invoice to me at MCA. You agreed, but the band was asked to pay at the reception desk.
I confirmed all these arrangements in writing after you agreed to them, so I simply do not understand the reason for these problems. I look forward to receiving your invoice with a large discount for the inconvenience that the band suffered. I would also like a letter of explanation and an apology.
Yours sincerely
Jem Stephens
Human Resources, MCA

Grammar backup 9

Reported speech

> ### Key
> **1b** He asked me if I had watched the awards ceremony the night before.
> **c** She told me (that) they had never been stopped in a security check there before.
> **d** He said that they were going to install satellite television the next day.
> **e** She asked us if we could contact her about the franchise later.
> **f** I told them (that) if we didn't leave soon, we would be late again.

Sound check

Running words together

Words ending in *t* or *d*

1 a Learners say the words. Play the tape for them to check their pronunciation.
b Copy the expressions onto the board. Play the tape. Discuss what happens to the final *t* and *d* sounds.
c Follow the same procedure as in **a**.
 *See Course Book.*

2 a Play the tape. Establish what happens to the final *t* and *d* sounds. Play the tape again. Learners listen and repeat.
b Follow the same procedure as in 1a.
 *See Course Book.*

Words ending in *n*

1 and 2 Follow the same procedure.
 See Course Book.

Market research

10A Consumers

> **Action**
>
> - Read about market research
> - Write questions
> - Carry out market research
> - Vocabulary and Grammar: phrasal verbs

Reading market research

1 As a class, name the items that are in the pictures and discuss the types of people who use them. Learners discuss the two questions in pairs and as a class.

2 Check learners understand *data*. Write **1–8** on the board. They read the stages and put them in the order they happen. Compare answers in pairs. Write the variations (using the letters) on the board, encouraging learners to use the sequencing words they studied on page 55. Leave their answers on the board for the next exercise.

3 Learners read the text and answer the questions. Check answers. Compare the answers for **c** with the learners's ideas on the board.

Key

1a suggested answer

trainers: Do you wear trainers? What brand of trainers do you wear? How much did they cost? Why did you buy the trainers you wear now? What does this brand in the picture mean to you? Have you seen them advertised? Do you know anyone who wears them? What do you think of people who wear these trainers?

b Interviews: face to face and by telephone; single and in groups. Questionnaire completion.

3a To find out the best places to advertise particular products to reach people who might be interested in certain kinds of product.

b Larger organisations.

c b, d, c, g, a, e, f, h

Vocabulary: phrasal verbs

4 Elicit examples of phrasal verbs that the learners know, e.g. *What do you do in the morning? (get up). What do you write at the end of a letter? (look forward to).* Copy the underlined words in the exercise onto the board. Read out sentence **a**. Ask learners to find the phrasal verb for *discover* in the text. Write **find out** on the board. Learners do the same for the other sentences. Compare answers in pairs and write them on the board. Establish that phrasal verbs cannot always be used as a substitute for the same verb, e.g. prepared: *I drew up the agenda for the meeting.* ✓ *I drew up a good meal last night.* ✗

Key

4a find out **b** drawn up **c** puts forward **d** carried out **e** sets up **f** take on **g** go ahead **h** put together

Grammar: phrasal verbs

5 **a** Direct learners to *'Companies carry out market research'* in the article. Establish that *carry out* is followed by an object. In pairs, learners decide if the other phrasal verbs are followed by an object or not. Check as a class.
b Discuss the question as a class.

6 Copy the first sentence onto the board. Together, decide where *this computer* can go. Learners do the same for the other sentences. Use the board to check their answers.

Key

5a carry out + market research; find out + what people think / answers; take on + a research agency; set up + meetings; puts forward + a market research plan / an easy-to-read report; go ahead (no object); draw up + object (in the text, it is in the passive form: a questionnaire is drawn up).

b The last sentence is incorrect because the object is a pronoun. It must be placed between the verb (*set*) and the particle (*up*).

6a Would you like to try (this computer) out (this computer)?

b If you've got a problem, can we talk it over?

c Can you please put them back?

d I'd like to put her forward for the manager's job.

e Can I write (your phone number) down (your phone number)?

Extra practice

P 10.1 Photocopy the worksheet on page 82. Make a set of cards for each group. Learners work in twos / threes. They deal out six cards each. The rest go in a pile, face down on the desk. Learners look at their cards but must not show them to the others. The first learner puts down a verb card on the table. The next learner puts a particle next to it that makes a phrasal verb and gives an example sentence. If the others think the example is wrong, the learner picks up another card. Then the next learner continues in the same way. If a learner cannot go, they pick up a card and miss a turn. The winner is the learner who uses all the cards first.

Writing and Speaking: market research

7 **a** Each learner chooses one of the products in Exercise 1. They use the headings to write questions for a market research interview.
b Learners work in pairs. **A** uses the questions from **a** to interview **B** about the product. Then they change roles. Correct any errors you hear at the end of the activity.

10B Keeping in touch

Action

- **Discuss ways of getting feedback**
- **Read a press release**
- **Talk about information in a table**
- **Read and write about the results of a survey**
- **Compare and contrast**
- **Vocabulary: marketing words**

Discussion: getting feedback

1 Learners look at the pictures and discuss the exercise. Find out if the learners have been on television, taken part in phone-ins, phoned a music station for a request, had a letter published in a newspaper etc. Ask learners to give examples of programmes that involve viewers.

Key

1 **suggested answers**
'Meet the viewers' events (e.g. music roadshows, concerts); phone-in programmes; inviting viewers to send things in (home videos, letters etc.); Internet pages.

Reading a press release

2 **a** Learners read the headline and discuss the question.
b–f Learners read the text and answer the questions. Check answers.

Key

2a the audience
b audience research and programme-making
c They probably helped to pay for the project in order to promote the company name to MTV viewers.
d It provided mobile film-making facilities for young people.
e Young people discussing issues that affect them.
f MTV: it produced a week of programmes and useful market research.
C&A: it associated the company name with a TV channel popular with young people.

Vocabulary: marketing words

3 Learners find the words in the text and match them with the definitions. Check answers.

Key

3a survey **b** event **c** project **d** promotion
e campaign

Reading and Speaking: describing the results of a survey

Write these three statements on the board:
- **School is a waste of time.**
- **Good school results help you to get a job.**
- **A degree is less useful than it used to be.**

Learners discuss the statements in small groups and as a class. Note how many people agree with each statement on the board. Learners then look at the survey and see how their views compare with the survey results.

4 **a** Learners look at the table and decide which statements are true or false. They correct the false ones. Check answers. Copy these expressions onto the board and highlight the form:
- **most + <u>people</u>**   • **<u>fewer</u> Poles <u>than</u> Germans**
- **a lot <u>of</u> + people**   •**17% <u>of</u> people**

b Each learner writes four statements about the table: make sure some of them are false. In pairs, they take it in turns to read out their sentences; their partner corrects the false ones. Alternatively, learners can write sentences in pairs and then read them out to another pair.

5 Learners match the survey extracts with the relevant section of the table. Check answers.

Key

4a • False. Only 12% of people think school is a waste of time.
• True.
• False. 77% of French people believe that a degree is less useful now than it used to be.
5 Text 1: Italy.
Text 2: the right-hand column (Degree less valuable than it used to be).

Vocabulary: common words in survey reports

6 Learners discuss the exercise in pairs. Write their answers on the board. Elicit the opposite of *on the one hand*. Learners look at the Phrasebook. Discuss the use of *far* and *slightly*.

Key

6a think, feel, believe
b although, whereas
c • not many: few
• most people: the majority
• the largest number of people: the highest percentage
• a much larger number of people: a far higher percentage

Writing: survey results

In pairs, learners write sentences using all the expressions in the Phrasebook. They swap their text with another pair to check for any errors.

8 Learners do the exercise individually or in pairs. It can be done for homework. For feedback, learners read each others' writing and decide which text is the most effective.

Key

7   suggested answer
GERMANY: On the one hand, about one-eighth of young people in Germany think that school is a waste of time. On the other hand, most people (86%) feel that success at school does help you to get a better job, although just over half believe a degree is less valuable than it used to be.

8   suggested answer
On average, 12% of people in Europe feel that school is a waste of time. The country with the highest percentage of people who feel this way is Poland (20%). In France, the figure is only slightly lower at 17%. The Dutch and Italians feel most positive about school education.

Extra practice

Learners work in small groups. Explain that the aim of the activity is to prove or disprove the statements about the other learners. First they write questions using the expressions in the Phrasebook, e.g. *Although most people watch TV every day, few of them listen to the radio. Slightly fewer people travel to work by bus than by car. The majority of people believe that everyone should retire at sixty.* Then they decide who is going to ask which questions and interview the other learners. If possible, give them time to interview other people outside class. Then they pool their information and write a short report of their findings to present to the class.

10C Behind the scenes

Action

- Talk about viewing figures
- Listen to an interview
- Interpret a chart
- Summarise information from a chart
- Vocabulary: audience research, collective nouns
- Grammar: *so / neither / nor*

Speaking: viewing figures

1 Discuss how much television the learners watch a week and when they watch it. They look at the viewing figures and discuss the exercise.

Key

1a The number of people (in millions) who watched the top five programmes on each channel.
b To sell advertising; to find out the times when most people are watching; to find out people's favourite types of programmes.

Listening: an interview

2 Learners listen to the tape and answer the questions. Check answers.

My job – I'm mainly responsible for Germany. I also deal with, like, UK and, I don't know, Italy, but the main focus is on Germany. Because I'm German and I know the market, or I should know the market … know what young people want. What we do is we get feedback from certain shows. We get the ratings, we get the viewing figures, and then we decide, does that show work in that time slot? Maybe we move it to another time slot … are we targeting the right audience at the right time with a certain show?
We've got, like, rating figures, or viewing figures over weekdays, Saturdays, Sundays for several months, weeks, whatever, so we plot them and you can see a graph from three o'clock in the morning to three o'clock the next morning and you can see where the peaks and where dips are. So you say OK that's performing well – high viewing figures, high ratings so that's OK. And if you do it for, let's say, weekly for say, four, five, six weeks and you always see at the same time that people are turning off, they're tuning out to watch something else. You think, hang on a minute and you look at this time slot. You look at how this time slot performed a year ago when a different show was on so you can see if it has improved or it's worse.
And, usually when we've got viewing figures, or ratings, or the weekly analysis of how a show's performed …. all that goes to the head of production, and to people who do the scheduling … er … music research people when it comes to the music issue.

Key

2a Germany. She is German and knows what young Germans are interested in.
b Viewing figures for certain programmes.
c To see whether programmes are succeeding or not - whether they are being shown at the right time to get the biggest audience, or whether they should be moved to a different time.
d The Head of Production, the people who do the scheduling, the music research people.
e **suggested answer**
The analysis of the figures provides a picture of how different programmes are performing and helps others to decide future programming.

Vocabulary: audience research

3 Learners do the exercise. Check answers.

Key

3a data, plot   **b** peaks, dips   **c** target
d time slot   **e** scheduling

Vocabulary: collective nouns

4 Write the two sentences in the exercise on the board. Establish that they are both grammatically correct. Discuss the difference in speaker perception of *audience*. In pairs, learners use the nouns in the box to make sentences using singular and plural verbs. Check answers.

Speaking: interpreting a chart

5 Learners discuss the exercise in pairs and as a class.

Key

5 suggested answers

The peak viewing hours are in the evening between 7 and 11. There is also a lower morning peak between 8 and 10. The show between 2 and 4 p.m. is doing very well with viewing figures rising. There are problems with the 8 to 10 p.m. slot. Figures are falling fast. It is important to point these things out quickly to the head of production.

Grammar: *so / neither / nor*

6 Learners discuss the exercise in pairs and as a class. Then copy this chart onto the board:

	agree	disagree
I like talk shows.		
He can't speak French.		

Read out the first sentence. Get learners to agree and disagree with you. Fill in **So do I. I don't!** Highlight the form. Do the same with the second sentence. Fill in **Nor can I. I can!**

7 Learners use the chart on the board to do the exercise. Check answers.

Key

6a They show that the same information is true for another slot.
 b *So:* when the information is positive. *Neither / nor:* when the information is negative.
 c The verb comes before the subject when we use *so* and *neither / nor.*
 The figures for the 6–7 slot remained the same.
 The figures for the 6–7 slot have not changed.
7a Neither / nor is the 12–1 slot.
 b So did the audience for the 9–10 slot.
 c Neither / nor have the programmes in the 9–10 slot.
 d So does the new 3 p.m. programme.

Extra practice

Learners work in small groups. Explain that they are going to test each other. Each group writes ten sentences, using a range of tenses and modal verbs (they can look at the Map of Book Units 1–10 to remind them of the different forms they have studied, or you can write them on the board, e.g. present perfect, *used to,* present simple). The first group reads out a sentence: the group which agrees / disagrees the quickest gets a point.

Speaking: describing a chart

8 If necessary, refer learners back to the language for interpreting data in the Phrasebook on page 50 or quickly brainstorm what they can remember on the board. Get a learner to read out the description of the chart. In pairs, they take it in turns to continue the description. For feedback, pairs describe the different time slots. If you wish, encourage learners to make notes as they listen. They can use them for the next exercise.

Key

8 suggested answer

... for example, the 11 a.m. slot and the 2–4 p.m. slots. The bad news is that audiences between 8 and 10 p.m. are falling steadily. Two other time slots should be watched carefully. There is a slight fall in the number of viewers between 4 and 5 p.m. and 5 and 6 p.m. A number of evening shows are holding their audience, with no increase or fall during September.

Writing: summarising information from a chart

9 Learners read the report. In pairs, they use their notes to write the second half. They swap their writing with another pair to see if it is the same.

Key

9 suggested answer

2 The 2–4 p.m. slot: The audience has risen steadily. Between 2 and 3 p.m. there has been an increase from about 1.3 million in the week beginning 1st September to 2 million by the end of the month. Viewing numbers for the 3–4 p.m. slot are up from 1.6 million to 2.4 million.
3 The 8–10 p.m. slot: This is a serious problem. Latest figures for each hour are 3.5 million, down from 6 million for the 8–9 p.m. slot and 6.3 million for the 9–10 slot.

Grammar backup 10

Phrasal verbs

Key

1b to find out **c** will put together **d** to draw up
 e to fill in **f** will set up **g** will take on
 h will put forward **i** will go ahead
2b This meeting is important. We must **set it up** as soon as possible.
 c Why don't we **go ahead with** interviews next week?
 d I'm sorry I haven't finished the report yet. I'll **put it together** this afternoon.

So / neither / nor

Key

1b Neither have we. **c** So did Cable Worldwide.
 d We can! **e** So am I. **f** Neither are the managers!
 g I think we should! **h** So should we.
2b So has Marina. **c** Neither / nor can Mr Woods.
 d Neither / nor will his secretary.
 e Neither / nor should you.
 f So did their colleagues.
 g So am I.
3a So can I / I can't. **b** So would I / I wouldn't.
 c Neither have I / I have. **d** Neither do I / I do.

11 At work

11A Working conditions

> ### Action
>
> - Read and talk about conditions of employment
> - Listen to an interview
> - Interview someone and report your findings
> - Vocabulary: working lives
> - Grammar: passive structures with *get*

Reading and Speaking: conditions of employment

1 Write **hours**, **holidays** and **pay** on the board. Learners read the two texts and make notes under the headings. In pairs, they compare notes and discuss the differences between working conditions in Britain and their country. Check as a class. Establish the difference between *a holiday* (British English, general word for rest from work, e.g. My next holiday is in June) and *holidays* (British English, for longer periods of rest, usually from school, e.g. Teachers get long summer holidays).

Vocabulary: working lives

2 **a** Copy the headings onto the board. Demonstrate the task with *pay*. In pairs, learners categorise the other words in the same way. Write their answers on the board, mark the stress and drill for correct pronunciation. See if learners can add any other words, e.g. perks, commission, shift work.
b Learners use the words to complete the text. Check answers.
c Learners discuss the exercise in pairs.

> #### Key
>
> **2a** • Employers: organisation, company, agency
> • Jobs: secretarial, clerical, administrative
> • Type of contract: part-time, full-time, temporary, permanent
> • Money: pay, wage, bonus, salary, hourly rate
> • Free time: holidays, day off, public holiday, break
> **b** 1 company / organisation / agency
> 2 administrative   3 part-time   4 holidays
> 5 public holidays   6 bonus / pay / salary

Listening to an interview

3 First discuss the possible differences between working in Germany and Britain and make notes on the board. Play the tape for learners to answer **a** and **b**. Check answers. Compare learners' ideas on the board with what Eva says. Discuss **c** as a class. Establish that *you know* and *I mean* are very common fillers but should not be over-used.

Again, I think that in the UK you can develop your career more easily in comparison to other countries. I mean in Germany it is quite normal to stay with a company for er, thirty five years until you retire ... and you do ....We have this expression, we

say you sit it out, you know, you just stay in your job and wait until eventually you get promoted. But this is changing now. In the UK you get promoted according to how you do the job. It's not so much about your age or how long you've been with a company. People can find jobs where they have a lot more power, a lot more responsibility. And they can earn much higher wages too. But it is hard to work in the UK, you know, working hours are sometimes very long. If you work in sectors like banking ... I know people who work till ten o'clock every night, lots of them, and they work weekends. That is totally crazy, I mean you don't do that in Germany. You might stay late now and then, and you might work the odd weekend, but there are people here that, you know, who don't do anything else except work. And then after ten years they are able to retire; after ten years they are where other people are when they are forty five and they're still only thirty. It is totally different here, totally different.

> #### Key
>
> **3a** Britain
> **b** Germany, Britain, Britain, Britain, Germany
> **c** To give herself time to think of what to say next; to clarify something by giving an example.

Grammar: passive structures with *get*

4 Copy the sentences onto the board. Discuss the exercise in pairs or as a class. Use the board to highlight answers. Establish that this structure is mainly used in spoken English.

5 Learners rewrite the sentences using *get*. Check answers.

> #### Key
>
> **4a** Someone pays you.   **b** You get a better job.
> **c** am, are   **d** past participle
> **5a** The offices don't get cleaned regularly.
> **b** She got sacked from the company last week.
> **c** Some of the computers got damaged in the move.
> **d** Our coats have got locked in the studio.
> **e** He got moved to a different department last week.
> **f** I get given all the difficult jobs.

Speaking and Writing: interviewing and reporting

6 First brainstorm questions for each heading in the exercise, e.g. *What hours do you work?* Ask learners to use the questions to interview you. Teach them *I'd rather not say* when they ask about your pay. Learners interview each other in pairs. If your learners do not have jobs, tell them to think of someone they know and answer for them. Make sure they make notes. They use the notes to write a report. For feedback, they read their report to the class.

7 Learners interview someone for homework. They report back to the class in a later lesson.

11B Working abroad

Action B

- Read an article
- Interview someone
- Read and write a CV and a letter of application
- Grammar: present perfect continuous

Reading: a magazine article

1 In pairs, learners look at the pictures and discuss the questions. Compare ideas but do not confirm them yet.

2 Learners read the text and check their answers to Exercise 1.

3 Learners read the text again and make notes under the four headings. Check answers.

Key

1a A flamenco dancer.
b Britain.
c In Estepona on the south coast of Spain.
d He works in Spain a lot, but tours the world with his company.
3 • education: He studied law and economics at university where he also continued studying the piano, violin and guitar.
• past jobs: solicitor
• present activities: touring the world with a flamenco and tango show
• skills: playing the violin, piano, guitar; dancing

Grammar: present perfect continuous

4 Copy these sentences onto the board:
I .... to flamenco festivals for many years.
We .... touring since 1995.
Learners complete the sentences. Then they check their answers in the text. Discuss the exercise as a class.

5 Learners read the CV and letter. Write **live in England?** on the board. Elicit the question and answer. Learners do the same for the other prompts. Ask pairs to read out the questions and answers.

Key

4a He started going many years ago and still goes now.
b They started in 1995 and are still doing the show now.
c *for* + period of time; *since* + point in time
d present tense of *have* + *been* + verb with *-ing*
e How long have you been going to flamenco festivals? How long have you been touring with Heartbeat?
f I've seen the best performers in Spain. We've been on three tours in Asia. We've given hundreds of performances. (The present perfect simple to talk about experiences that happened sometime in the past.) I've been accepted by the flamenco community in Estepona. (The present perfect simple to talk about a state / experience that happened in the past and is still true now.)

5a How long has she been playing in an orchestra? Since 1995.
b How long has she been working for UKTV? Since 1998.
c How long has she been working as a senior researcher? Since 1998.
d How long has she been counselling young people? For two years.

Extra practice

P 11.1 Photocopy the worksheet on page 83. Learners work in pairs. First they read their letter and complete half the chart with their information. Then they interview their partner and complete the other half.

Key

	Véronique	David
Where is (s)he living now?	Hong Kong	Hamburg
How long has (s)he been living there?	2 months	2 years
Where did (s)he live before?	London	Oxford
How long did (s)he live there?	3 years	20 years
Why is (s)he saving?	to buy a flat	to buy a BMW
How much has (s)he saved this year?	£5,000	£6,000
How much did (s)he save last year?	£10,000	£2,000
How much did (s)he save the year before?	£15,000	£4,000
How long has (s)he been saving?	3 years	2 years
How much has (s)he saved up to now?	£30,000	£12,000

Speaking: interviews

6 Learners copy the headings in Anne's CV into their notebooks. If necessary, list the questions they will need to ask on the board. In pairs, they interview each other and complete their partner's CV. Correct any errors you hear at the end of the exercise.

Writing a letter of application

7 Learners discuss the exercise. Find out if they write letters of application in the same way in their countries.

8 First learners write their CV. Then they write a letter of application. This exercise can be done for homework. If you wish, get learners to apply for the same job. Then they read each others' letters and decide which four learners should be short-listed for an interview.

Key

7a Paragraph 1: states purpose of the letter; paragraph 2: gives details of experience; paragraph 3: concludes the letter.
b Yours faithfully: polite way to end a letter to someone whose name you do not know. Yours sincerely: polite way to end a letter addressed to a person by name.

11C Interviews

Action

- **Read a job advertisement**
- **Talk about interviews**
- **Listen to an extract from a talk on interview techniques**
- **Listen to an extract from a job interview**
- **Interview someone**
- **Present yourself**
- **Vocabulary: personal qualities**

Reading a job advertisement

1 Learners read the advertisements and answer the questions. Check answers.

2 Learners discuss the exercise in small groups and as a class.

3 Brainstorm other adjectives to describe personal qualities. Write them on the board. Learners discuss the exercise in pairs. Compare their ideas as a class. If you wish, use the adjectives to describe the learners' jobs or ones they would like to have. Establish which adjectives have nouns and what they are, e.g. *enthusiastic – enthusiasm*.

Key

1a Keycamp Holidays **b** temporary, full-time
  c Campsite courier: to look after people staying on the camp.
  Children's courier: to look after and organise activities for children staying at the campsite.
  Site supervisor / senior courier: to supervise the work of all the couriers on the site.
  d Independent, sociable and enthusiastic people who can speak several languages.
  e Write to or telephone Keycamp to ask for further details and an application form.

Extra practice
Elicit opposites of the adjectives in Exercise 3, e.g. *enthusiastic – unenthusiastic, independent – dependent*. In pairs, learners use the adjectives to describe themselves and members of their family.

Speaking: interviews

4 Discuss the exercise in pairs or as a class.

Listening: interview techniques

5 **a** Learners discuss the question in pairs or as a class.
  b Learners listen to Alison and make notes under the headings. Check answers.
  c and d Discuss as a class.

You can prepare for interviews and it is possible to improve your interviewing style. The first thing you should do is to find out as much as you can about the company and the job itself. The interviewers will be impressed if you have done some homework on the company. It shows initiative. I always tell people to imagine themselves in the interviewer's situation.

What kind of person are they looking for? How many of those skills and qualities do you have? And how can you demonstrate them as effectively as possible?
It is vital to have clear strategies for an interview. How you present yourself is important – the clothes you wear, your body language, the way you speak, how much you smile. You should also look enthusiastic – as if you really are interested in the job. All of these affect an interviewer's decision. The way you speak is particularly important. It is almost always a mistake to talk too much, but speaking too little can also be a problem. You have to be sensitive to the situation. Remember that the interviewer is in control and you should not try to take that control away. But at the same time no interviewer is looking for one-word answers to questions. Most interviewers give you a chance to ask questions at the end, and you should definitely use that opportunity. But again, not too many questions – the interviewers probably only have a few minutes before they need to see someone else!

Key

5b • Preparing: find out about the company and the job; think about the skills and qualities they will be looking for.
  • Appearance: your clothes, body language, smiling and enthusiasm are important.
  • Speaking: try not to talk too much or too little.
  • Questions: ask some questions at the end but not too many.

Listening to an extract from a job interview

6 Check learners understand *initiative* and *strategies*. Remind learners of the three jobs in Exercise 1. They listen to the interview once and answer **a**. Play the interview again for them to answer **b** and **c**. Check answers. Discuss **d** as a class.

 Well, first of all I've got quite a lot of experience of the leisure industry. As you know, I've worked in hotels for the last two summers. Er ... and I've had experience of working abroad – one of the hotels was in the south of France, near Nice. I've also got a background in working with young people. You know – from my CV – that I helped to run my local youth club ... and at the hotel last year I managed the reception desk, so I was responsible for the other receptionists. Then there's my training. I've been studying business management so I understand any business aspects of the job. I'm good with computers. I'm familiar with different software packages ... word-processing, databases and spreadsheets. My foreign languages are not too bad – I can manage in French and Spanish and I'm learning German.
On the personal side, I think I'm good at working with people ... you know, as part of a team ... but I can also work alone. I'm hard-working ... well-organised ... and enthusiastic ... I know clients can be difficult, but people tell me I'm very diplomatic.

> **Key**
>
> **6a** site supervisor / senior courier
>   **b** • personal qualities: 'On the personal side...'
>   • skills: 'Then there's my training.'
>   • experience: 'Well, first of all, I've got quite a lot of experience.'
>   **c** • education: he has studied business management and knows some languages.
>   • foreign language skills: he has a reasonable knowledge of French and Spanish, and is learning German.
>   • leadership skills: he has helped to run a youth club and has been responsible for receptionists in a hotel.
>   **d** Yes, he seems to have the right kind of experience.

Speaking: interviewing

Learners look at the Phrasebook and listen to the interview in Exercise 6 again. They tick the expressions they hear. In pairs, they take it in turns to use the expressions to talk about themselves.

7 a If you wish, replace the job advertisement in the exercise with one which is relevant to the learners' work experience. Divide learners into groups of four and then into two pairs. They read the information about the roles. Learners roleplay the conversation: make sure **A** begins with *Why do you think you're suitable for the job?* Note down any errors you hear.
b They change partners and roleplay the same conversation. Finally the four learners discuss whether the applicants were suitable or not.

Grammar backup 11

Passive structures with *get*

> **Key**
>
> **1b** get married   **c** get changed   **d** get invited
>   **e** get dressed   **f** got stopped   **g** got lost
>   **h** get paid   **i** didn't get stolen   **j** going to get promoted
>   **k** got damaged   **l** got caught

Present perfect continuous

> **Key**
>
> **1b** had a meeting for a long time.
>   **c** has had three driving lessons.
>   **d** been flying with British Airways for ten years.
>   **e** known him for six years.
> **2b** She's been going to international conferences **for** two years.
>   **c** We **have been** working late every night this week.
>   **d** I **have lived** in London since 1978 and I'll never move.
>   **e** He's been **working** here for two years.
>   **f** They haven't **reached** a decision yet.

12 In the news

12A Presenting

Action

- Talk about presenting news
- Listen to an interview
- Read about a person's career path
- Talk about work experience
- Grammar: past perfect

Speaking: presenting news

1 Discuss how learners find out about the news, e.g. via TV, radio, newspapers. Learners discuss the exercise in pairs or as a class.

Listening to an interview

2 **a** Learners look at the photograph and read about Thomas Madvig. They discuss the question. Do not confirm their ideas yet.
b Play the tape for learners to check their answers.

I work as a presenter ... for news. I write them ... I work as a writer as well as a researcher and as a producer on packages, cutting, editing, interviewing ... and so I do the whole sort of newsroom bit ... yeah, I do all round everything basically. There's nothing I don't do there ... so writing, producing, presenting I think would sum it up. I'm basically hired as a presenter and a journalist ... and so journalist functions as well ... without, sort of, having experience as one ... but that's the job.
It's sort of young people's news. So that it works as a news channel for young people. If there's a youth problem or big youth demonstration in Germany we've got the footage of, we'll get the story and that's important news for us. So it's just like ... I think it's like major news except for it's for 15 to 25 year olds. So we don't go for the big international things unless it's involving young people.
We have an editor, we have an editor-in-chief, and then we have a music editor ... the main editor ... we have a morning meeting ... the work procedure is that we meet at nine and go through papers, wires, sources, stories, radio, everything. Ten fifteen we have a morning meeting like a normal news department with ... er ... all come out with our stories and then we discuss them and find out if they're worth taking up. After that we get assigned two or three stories each and ... and from there the day goes on with a deadline at three ... researching and finding the stories and writing them up, or how much is on getting graphics in and everything ...

3 Play the tape again for learners to answer the questions. Check answers.

Key

2b edits, researches, writes, interviews, finds graphics
3a MTV news is specifically for young people, 15–25 year olds.
b newspapers, wires, radio
c two or three
d three o'clock

Reading: a career path

4 In pairs, learners order the sentences chronologically. Compare ideas as a class. Then they read the text to check their answers.

Key

4 c, e, b, d, a, f

Grammar: past perfect

5 Write these two sentences on the board:
- **When Thomas first ..... (come) to London, he ..... (do) just about everything he could.**
- **I ..... (know) about music, and I ..... (write) quite a lot.**
Learners complete the sentences and then check their answers in the text. Discuss the exercise in pairs or as a class. Draw this timeline on the board:

Refer learners to the first example sentence on the board. Establish which parts of the sentence the two crosses refer to.

6 Check learners understand *voice-over*. Ask two learners to read out the example exchange. In pairs, learners do the same with the other prompts. For feedback, volunteer pairs roleplay their exchanges: the other learners check they are correct.

Key

5a We use the past perfect to refer to an activity that happened before a particular time in the past.
b past tense of *have* + past participle
6a Had he worked in television? No, he hadn't.
b Had he presented radio programmes? Yes, he had.
c Had he done voice-overs? Yes, he had.
d Had he written reviews? Yes, he had.
e Had he presented TV programmes? No, he hadn't.
f Had he read the news in Danish? Yes, he had.
g Had he written news items in English? No, he hadn't.
h Had he been a DJ in different countries? No, he hadn't.

Speaking: work experience

7 First learners note down four key dates / events in their lives on slips of paper, e.g. 1986 – went to America, 1988 – left school. They swap these pieces with their partner who asks questions about what happened before, e.g. *Had you been to America before? Had you travelled abroad before?* They note down their partner's answers and then report back to the class, e.g. *Nicole went to America in 1986. She hadn't been before.* Correct any errors you hear with the past simple and past perfect.

Extra practice

P 12.1 Photocopy the story on page 84. In pairs, learners read it and fill in the missing verbs. For feedback, each pair reads out their versions. The pairs with the same verbs as below get a point.

Key

a hadn't heard   b had missed   c had left
d had organised   e had been closed   f had gone
g had forgotten

12B Getting it right

Action

- **Talk about foreign language use**
- **Read an interview extract**
- **Read information from a news agency**
- **Write and present a news report**
- **Grammar: extended noun phrases**

Speaking: foreign languages

1 Discuss the differences between speaking and writing English and what learners find easy / difficult about each skill. They discuss Thomas's opinions in pairs and as a class.

Reading an interview extract

2 Learners discuss the exercise in pairs. Do not confirm their answers yet.

3 **a** Learners read the text and check their answers to Exercise 2. **b and c** Learners read the text again and answer the questions. Check answers. Then learners write down two things they are good at in English and two things they need to improve. Compare ideas in pairs and as a class. If you wish, do the Learning Skills on page 137 to give learners ideas on how to improve their English outside the classroom.

Key

3a Yes, it is. He writes scripts for news items.
b He has a good voice and good pronunciation.
c Grammar.

Reading information from a news agency

4 Check learners understand *news agency* (e.g. Reuters) and *ashes*. Learners read the text and answer the questions. Check answers.

5 Follow the same procedure as Exercise 4.

Key

4a It's the first funeral to take place in space. It involved two famous people.
b From a Lockheed–1011 plane over the Canary Islands.
c USA (Celestis is in Houston).
d In September for $4,800.
5a The two celebrities. To attract listeners' attention.
b There are fewer sentences. Each sentence contains more information than in the first text. Information that will attract listeners is mentioned early on. Information about the company is much later. The radio text contains a lot of extended noun phrases.

Grammar: extended noun phrases

6 Write **Gene Roddenberry** on the board and elicit the other words that are used before it. Do the same with the other main nouns. Discuss **b** as a class.

7 Write the first sentence in the exercise on the board. As a class, rewrite the first part with an extended noun phrase. Learners do the same with the other sentences. Check answers.

8 Demonstrate the task with *manager*: ask two learners to take it in turns to read out the example. In pairs, learners do the same with the other nouns. For feedback, they read out their sentences: the pair with the longest and most logical extended noun phrase / sentence gets a point.

Key

6a Gene Roddenberry; Timothy Leary; funeral; Celestis. Other words that come before these nouns are nouns and adjectives.
b To include a lot of information in a very short news report.
7a Hollywood film start Brad Pitt …
b his forty-year old French girlfriend …
c London-based MTV Europe …
d A Eurasia Airways Boeing 737 …
e People's Bank investment services …

Writing and Speaking: presenting a news report

9 If you wish, brainstorm current local or national events which are in the news. Write them on the board. Learners work in small groups and choose three of the events to include in their report. Make sure they decide who is going to read which part of the report. They practise reading it first in their groups. Then they present it to the whole class.

12C Editing skills

Action

- Talk about reasons for writing
- Recognise types of mistake
- Improve a letter and fax
- Write a fax from notes

Speaking: reasons for writing

1 Discuss the exercise as a class.

Reading: types of mistake

2 Write **A–F** on the board. In pairs, learners find the mistakes in the text and categorise the type of mistakes. Write their corrections on the board.

3 Learners read the checklist and answer **a–c**. Check answers. Then discuss **d** and **e** as a class.

Key

2 A have (has) – grammar
   B invoise (invoice) – spelling
   C Its (It's) – punctuation
   D Westmoor St 14 (14 Westmoor St.) – organisation
   E Hello Mr Jones (Dear Mr Jones) – style
   F bring (send) – vocabulary

3a Because these are the most important areas.
 b Vocabulary, spelling, punctuation and grammar.
 c Because they are to do with correctness rather than choice. In the first stages of writing, you choose what you want to write and how you want to say it. In the last stages, you check that you have used the correct form.

Writing: improving letters and faxes

4 In pairs, learners use the checklist in Exercise 3 to improve the letter. If you wish, write a correct version on the board with the learners' help.

5 Follow the same procedure as Exercise 4.

6 Each learner writes a fax to Mr Barnett using the message in Text 3. Then they exchange faxes and use the checklist to improve their partner's writing.

Key

4 **suggested answer**

GKT International
Bahnhofstrasse, 12
München
December 12th

Dear Mr Barnett,
Thank you for your letter of December 8th.
I have spoken to our UK representative, Patrick Donaldson, and asked him to contact you as soon as possible about arranging a meeting. He has samples of all our products and promotional material and will be very interested in discussing future possibilities with you.
I enclose some information about the company and look forward to hearing from you soon.
Yours sincerely,
George Stakis

5 **suggested answer**
FAX
To: Josef Pesti, GKT, Tallinn
From: George Stakis
Date: December 22nd
Pages: 1
Re: Visit to Tallinn

I will be in Tallinn on Wednesday, January 4th. My plane arrives at 16.30 – a Lufthansa flight from Munich.
Could you please book a hotel for me for Wednesday and Thursday nights and meet me at the airport?
Best wishes,
George Stakis

Grammar backup 12

Past perfect

Key

1b had tested, tried   c crashed, remembered, had received
 d bought, was   e arrived, had disappeared
 f told, had asked   g looked, saw, had made
 h asked, was, had answered

Extended noun phrases

Key

1b Internationally famous scuba diving champion, Denise Swan, announced her retirement yesterday after twenty years in the sport.
 c Top British fashion designer, Angela Lawrence, has just launched her own range of children's clothes.
 d Thompsons latest market research figures show that most British households now own at least two television sets.
 e Mail order company Computer Games is one of the fastest growing companies in Britain.
 f Multi-lingual senior sales manager, Simon Ronson, has made history by negotiating a contract in three languages.
 g The growing Spanish tourist industry is a result of tour operators reducing their prices by 20%.

2b Statistics show students find the Australian university entrance exam very difficult to pass.
 c You need to go to the airport lost luggage department because we cannot find your suitcase.
 d Famous American singer Janet Jackson has just arrived in London for the start of her world tour.

13A Intra

Action

- Read an introduction to a company
- Compare marketing methods
- Grammar: linking words

Reading an introduction to a company

To introduce the company, refer learners to the two pictures. They list the things they would like to find out about Intra. Write their questions on the board, e.g. **What kind of company is it? What does it do?** Then they read the text and find which questions are answered. Ask if any of the learners know anything about any similar companies.

1 **a** Learners read the text and write an explanation (maximum 20 words) of what Intra does. Compare in pairs.
b Discuss the question.

2 This second reading task aims to stimulate discussion – the text does not explicitly supply answers to the questions. Learners read the text again and discuss the questions in pairs and as a class.

Key

suggested answers

1a Intra helps companies to create an image and to promote their products through traditional and interactive media.
b Young, lively, modern, up-to-date.
2a • A Web site gives up-to-date information about a company and its activities. It offers an interactive facility for communicating with potential customers.
• An Internet address allows people to find the Web site and to e-mail the company.
• A database stores details on a computer such as names, addresses, products bought so that they can be easily called up.
b traditional: magazines and newspapers; direct marketing by mail; telephone
interactive: the World Wide Web, telemarketing
both: television (e.g. shopping channel); radio
c By including a facility that allows feedback from clients / customers / listeners etc., e.g. a radio programme can become interactive by including a phone-in slot; a newspaper can print readers' letters or hold events which bring it into contact with its readers. A Web site is non-interactive if it just provides information, but becomes interactive if people can e-mail it, respond to it or change it in some way.

Grammar: linking words

Write this sentence on the board:
I like learning English but . . .
Elicit learners' ideas and complete the sentence. Discuss the function of *but*. Ask learners to read the text in Exercise 1 again and find words which have the same function as *but*. Check

answers. Then they read the sentences in Exercise 3 to see if they have found them all.

3 Learners discuss the exercise in pairs. Use the board to check their answers.

4 Do **a** together as a class. Establish that *although* can be replaced by *but* if *although* is in the middle of the sentence. Learners do the same for the other sentences. Check answers.

Key

3a They introduce a contrast between two clauses.
b The first sentence. *But* usually comes in the middle of a sentence and introduces the second clause.
c *despite / in spite of* + verb with *-ing*
Although they are in the far north of Europe, Swedish companies can reach a global audience.
d despite the fact that
4a Although our offices are both in Sweden, we have international contacts through an association of marketing agencies in Brussels. / Our offices are both in Sweden although we have international contacts through an association of marketing agencies in Brussels.
b The association is in Brussels, but its correspondence is usually in English.
c While some of our clients are only interested in Swedish customers, they will reach a global audience if they advertise in English.
d Despite working mainly in Swedish, I need English when I search for information on the Internet. / Despite the fact that I work mainly in Swedish, I need English when I search for information on the Internet.
e Though Web site design is interesting, it is difficult to work on a small screen format. / Web site design is interesting though it is difficult to work on a small screen format.
f In spite of being Swedish-speaking, some of our Finnish clients prefer to write to us in English. / In spite of the fact that many of our Finnish clients are Swedish-speaking, some prefer to write to us in English.

Extra practice

P 13.1 Photocopy the worksheet on page 84 (if you have a large class, make several copies). Divide the sentence halves among the learners: make sure they get an equal number of beginnings and endings. They mingle, read out their beginnings and find the other halves. They keep the beginning and give away the ending. For feedback, they read their sentences and the others check that they are correct.

Speaking: comparing marketing methods

5 Copy this chart onto the board:

	advantages for customers	advantages for advertisers
TV ads		
Web site		

Learners write an advantage in each box. They compare ideas in pairs, then two pairs compare together and so on. Finally discuss as a class.

13B The Internet

Action

- Talk about the Internet
- Read Web site pages
- Listen to a talk on Web site design
- Read and write messages
- Vocabulary: computer commands

Speaking: using the Internet

Write **the Internet** on the board and find out what the learners think of / feel when they see the word and why.

1 Learners discuss the exercise in pairs and as a class.

Key

1a suggested answers
search for information, go shopping, get free software, advertise, ask for help, send e-mail messages

Vocabulary: computer commands

2 Check learners understand *icon*. Write **A–K** on the board. Demonstrate the task: ask *Which icon is for print?* Write **print** next to **F** on the board. Learners label the other icons in the same way. Check answers. Elicit other commands the learners know, e.g. *merge, download, delete, click on, highlight.*

3 Learners complete the sentences. Check answers.

Key

2 A connect B search C paste D cut E open F print
G save H undo I copy J view K help
3a connect **b** help **c** undo **d** view **e** copy / cut, paste

Extra practice

If your learners use computers regularly, ask them the questions below. In pairs, they write the process with as few words as possible. For feedback they read out their answers. The pair with the shortest and clearest description gets a point.
1 How do you move text? 2 How do you delete text?
3 How do you open a file? 4 How do you close a file?
5 How do you underline a 6 How do you print a document?
   word?

Reading Web site pages

Check learners know what Addison Wesley Longman ELT is. Discuss what learners would like to find in the AWL Web site. Then look at the Web site information on page 105 and see if it gives them what they want.

4 Learners discuss the exercise.

Key

4a A magazine is a user-friendly way to organise a site. Users are familiar with this way of reading. They can go straight to the part of the site that interests them. It is a like a magazine in that it has a contents page.
b Monthly. 'More prizes to be won this month.'
c 3 – because you can ask questions; 5 – because you can do a competition; 7 – because you can go anywhere else on the Web site.

Listening and Speaking: designing Web sites

5 Direct learners to the chart. Demonstrate the task: ask *Which category will you choose to find information on More Work in Progress?* Elicit *catalogue / new titles.* In pairs, learners do the same for the prompts. Check answers.

6 Play the tape for learners to answer **a–c**. Check answers and discuss **d**. If learners have access to the Internet, encourage them to go into the AWL Web site. They can send their views on the site and on *More Work in Progress* to AWL via *'talk to us'.*

(S = Sara I = interviewer)
s: *For a company trying to do business on the Internet, the design of your Web site is extremely important. And when I talk about design I don't just mean producing something that looks nice. A site is well-designed if it works ... that is, it does three key things. First of all it attracts people to look at it – without that you've failed. The second is that it keeps the viewer interested ... keeps them coming back for more visits. And finally, the purpose of all company Web sites at the end of the day ... it must help you sell your product or your service. All company Web sites try to achieve these three aims.*
I: *So how can you design a Web site so that people want to keep visiting it?*
s: *Well ... the introductory page is important. So many companies just put pages on the Web and leave them there. If you look at it in December you find it hasn't changed at all since six months earlier. You must maintain a Web site, and one of the best ways of encouraging repeat visits is to keep changing the introductory page – provide up-to-date information, focus on different products, give visitors something new to see and do. I mean, it's a bit like a newspaper – when you've read a newspaper once you don't go back and have another look at it the following week, do you? We want to read about something different. It's the same with a Web site.*
I: *What about the content of a Web site? What general advice can you give to someone setting up a Web site for the first time?*
s: *Good Web sites are separated into different pages. Every page should, of course, contain the company name and a way of contacting them. It should also provide a list of what is available on the other pages and an easy way of moving from one page to another ... maybe some sort of map of the site where you can click on the other pages.*
I: *OK, but what about the actual information on the site?*
s: *Well, let's take an example. A record company, for instance. It will have information about the company's products – a catalogue of some sort. It may have a group of pages that provides background information on its artists. It may allow you to listen to particular pieces of music and perhaps see video clips. It will certainly have a*

contact page, which allows you to e-mail the company and perhaps order its products. They may even have a chatline, a forum that allows you to ask questions to your favourite star and perhaps even get replies. There could be quizzes, competitions, special offers. There's no limit, really.

Key

5a new titles / catalogue **b** talk to us **c** talk to us
d register **e** Asia outlook **f** look who's talking
g jobs **h** AWL map
6a They should: attract people to look at them; keep people interested so that they visit the site regularly; help you to sell your product or service.
b Keep changing and updating the introductory page so that it's different each time people visit the site.
c It should contain: the company name and how to contact them on each page; a list of all pages and a way of moving easily between them; information pages about products with the opportunity to see some of them and order them; opportunities for interaction, e.g. via a chatline, quizzes, competitions, special offers.

Reading and writing messages

Learners read message A. Establish what Kurt Blocker wants to know. Then learners read message B. Elicit Sara's answers.

7 a Learners write an answer to message A with information about their own country.
b Learners write a message with questions about a country that they would like to work in. If you have learners from different countries, they can write a message about working in that country for another learner to answer.

13C The widening gap

Action

■ **Read and talk about fear of technology**
■ **Talk about things you do and do not regret**
■ **Grammar: third conditional sentences**

Reading and Speaking: fear of technology

1 Find out if learners' attitudes to computers are the same as their parents'. Check learners understand *techno fear*. Learners look at the chart and answer **a** and **b**. Check answers and discuss **c** and **d**.

2 Learners read the article and answer **a–c**. Check answers and discuss **d** as a class.

Key

1a More men than women own computers. More young people own computers than older ones.
b Computer ownership is growing fast. The gap between computer use by men and women is growing. The number of elderly people (over 65) using computers is falling.
c **suggested answers**
Men have more money than women? Men have always been more interested in computers than women? Younger people are more likely to try, and have access to new technology than older people?
2a It will divide into those who have access to information and those who do not.
b Ron is really interested in computers and has all the latest computer equipment; Susie is not interested in computers and doesn't have any equipment.
c She's afraid that her lack of computer knowledge will damage her career.

Grammar: third conditional sentences

3 Books closed. Ask the class the questions in **a**. Then ask *What does Ron say?* Elicit a third conditional sentence and write it on the board. Do the same with **b**. Discuss **c** and **d**. Highlight the weak forms and contractions on the board and drill for correct pronunciation.

4 Learners use the information in the text about Lottie to complete the sentences. Check answers.

Key

3a Yes. Yes.
b No. No.
c We use third conditional sentences to talk about events or situations which are completely in the past and cannot be changed. We are imagining the opposite of what actually happened.
d *If* + past perfect clause + *would have* + past participle.
4a she wouldn't have stayed at school for an extra year.
b she wouldn't have been able to go to college to study business administration.
c if she hadn't gone to England for three months to improve her English.
d she wouldn't have gone to England / she would have got the job the first time.
e if she hadn't got the job in the hotel.

Speaking: regrets ... no regrets

Books closed. To introduce the language, copy this onto the board:

<u>Regrets</u>

I wish I hadn't	harder.
If only I'd stayed	to get angry.
I'm sorry I didn't work	not taking that job.
It's a pity I didn't	shouted at him.
I regret	in my home town.
I was wrong	listen to her.

<u>No regrets</u>

I'm glad	to get some extra qualifications.
I don't regret	I left when I did.
I was absolutely right	taking that job.

In pairs, learners match the sentence halves. Books open. They look at the Phrasebook to check their answers. Highlight the form on the board.

5 Each learner lists two things they regret doing and two things they are glad they did. Read out the examples in the exercise. Learners write similar sentences using their lists. They read out their sentences to the class.

Extra practice

Divide learners into two groups. Read the story once to the learners. Then read it again, pausing for them to write sentences using the expressions in the Phrasebook and the third conditional: one group writes what Chris is thinking and the other group does the same for Helen. They read out their sentences. The group with the most (correct) sentences wins.

Story

Chris and Helen have just had a difficult meeting with some clients. It started badly when Chris arrived half an hour late / because he left the office late. / Unfortunately there had been a lot of traffic / although the underground trains were working fine. / When the meeting started, Helen discovered that the figures in the quote were wrong because she hadn't checked her secretary's typing. / The clients said she was incompetent / and she lost her temper with them. / Then Chris remembered that he had brought the latest market research data with him which had some of the figures in it. / As the meeting was ending and Chris was putting on his coat, he spilt a glass of water over the Managing Director / but Chris apologised so much, that the Managing Director said he didn't mind. / They're now on their way back to the office. What are they both thinking?

Grammar backup 13

Linking words

Key

1b despite the fact that   c Although
 d despite   e While
2b Although   c Despite the fact
 d In spite of   e While   f though
3b Although he didn't have any money, he went on holiday.
 c In spite of getting up very early, she missed her flight.
 d While we tried hard, we weren't able to complete the job.

Third conditional sentences

Key

1b If the spare parts hadn't arrived late, we could have delivered them.
 c If we hadn't worked until midnight, we wouldn't have finished the job.
 d He could have written the report if you'd asked him.
 e She would have gone to the meeting if her car hadn't broken down on the motorway.
2a studied harder at school.
 b made so much noise last night.
 c phoned you if I'd got your number.
 d given me promotion, I wouldn't have left the company.
3b If they **had** placed their order earlier, they would have received the machines by now.
 c She would **have** got the job if her English had been better.
 d If we had **had** a stand at the exhibition, we might have won their order.
 e If I hadn't gone to the conference in Vienna, I wouldn't have **met** my future employer.
 f I wish I **had** saved more money when I was working.
 g What **would you have** done if you had been me?

Our environment

14A Policies

Action

- **Discuss environmental problems**
- **Listen to an interview**
- **Listen and take notes**
- **Write from notes**
- **Make recommendations**
- **Vocabulary: resources**

Speaking: environmental problems

1 Learners describe what they can see in the pictures. Help them with any new vocabulary. Then they discuss the exercise in pairs or as a class.

2 Learners discuss the exercise. Find out what kind of environmental damage they have in their country. Check they understand *recycled, poisonous, harmful.*

Key

1a They are: polluting the air; making noise; creating possible hazards

b litter; smoking; wastage (paper etc.)

c recycle; cut down on waste

2 • environmental policy: a plan of ways to have as little damaging effect on the environment as possible.
  • goals: things that you hope to do by a future time.
  • environmental damage: harm to the air, water, earth, plants, animals, people etc. around us.

Listening to an interview

3 Establish what Bjorn Falkanäs does. Learners listen to the tape and answer the questions. Check answers.

🔊 *What we have done so far is that we have made up our own environmental policy. We look at how we use, for example, energy, how we sit when we work, what we use for chemicals, how we transport people, how we transport films – everything. And what we try to do is to set goals for causing less environmental damage. So we make the right choice every time we have to, for instance, decide about transport – to transport by train or by bicycle, and so on. We write down how we do things today and what our goals are for the next year. We have already made some changes. For instance, we use a lot of chemicals and plastic film in our reproduction process, and now we have new green film which is less hard on the environment and the chemicals we use are recycled. We choose print companies that do not use harmful, poisonous colours. We employ a consultant to drive this project and she helps us to ask the right questions. We do this because we care about our environment, but it's also very important for our relationship with customers. And we look at how our partners work – do they have an environmental policy? If they don't, we can't work with them.*

Key

3a They have introduced an environmental policy for the company, e.g. they use a different kind of film and recycle chemicals. They use print companies who do not use poisonous colours.

b She helps them to direct their policy.

c Intra cares about the environment and it is important for their relationship with their customers.

d They don't work with companies who don't have an environmental policy. This encourages the companies to take environmental matters seriously.

Vocabulary: resources

4 Copy the headings onto the board. Demonstrate the task with *boxes*. In pairs, learners categorise the words. Write their answers on the board, mark the stress and drill for correct pronunciation. Leave them there for the next exercise.

5 **a** Copy this chart onto the board.

positive	negative

Follow the same procedure as in Exercise 4. Establish that the prefix *re* means again.

b Refer learners back to the resources on the board. In pairs, learners use the adjectives in Exercise 5 to describe the resources. Compare answers.

Key

4 energy: heating, electricity (gas, solar power)
transport: lorries, trains (ships, planes)
materials: paint, chemicals (plastic, metal)
packaging: boxes, polystyrene (cardboard, crates)

5 positive: recyclable, reusable, environmentally-friendly, safe, renewable, clean, green
negative: harmful, poisonous, noisy, toxic, damaging, wasteful, polluted, dirty

Listening and Writing: taking notes

6 **a** Check learners understand *raw material*. Play the tape for them to complete the chart. Check answers.

b Learners listen again to note down the expressions. Check answers.

🔊 *We're here today to talk about business and the environment. Well, every company needs to consider the following three key areas. Firstly, input – in other words, the resources that we use … the things we need to do our work, to make products or provide services. Secondly, the process, or what we do with those resources in the workplace – the way we use them. And lastly, the output from our business – and by output I mean the products and waste materials that are the results of our work. So what can we do to cause as little damage as possible to the environment? Well, we can look at the things we buy and see if there are better alternatives. If there are, then we need to*

persuade suppliers to provide them. And they may be able to use less packaging too, if we ask them to.
Next, within our workplaces, we need to use our resources efficiently, so there's no waste. We can, for example, switch off office machines that are not in use, and we can make sure that delivery vans only leave when they are full.
Then, output. Well, how much waste is really necessary? We must ask ourselves if it's recyclable. Or could another company use it as a raw material for its products? If these options are not possible, then we must dispose of the waste safely.

Key

6a B PROCESS = what we do with the resources. • Use them efficiently, cut down waste.
C OUTPUT. • Recycle waste if possible or dispose of it safely.
  b • Firstly, secondly, next, then, lastly
  • in other words, or, by (output) I mean

Writing from notes

7 Learners use their notes and the expressions from Exercise 6 to write a short report. This exercise can be done in pairs or for homework.

Key

7 suggested answer
. . . or the resources we use. Companies should look for better resources, and persuade suppliers to provide them. We can also try to persuade suppliers to use less packaging.
Secondly, companies should look at process, the way those resources are used. Can we cut down on waste by using the resources more efficiently? We should, for example, switch off machines that are not in use, and fill delivery lorries before they leave.
The last area is output, in other words the company's products and waste materials. Waste should be recycled if possible, and another company may be able to use it as a raw material. If recycling is not possible, we must consider how to dispose of the waste safely.

Extra practice

Copy these stress patterns onto the board. In small groups, learners list all the words they can remember from 14A to do with the environment, plus ones which they used in their discussions. The group with the most words under the correct patterns wins.
- ■ (safe, clean, green, waste)
- ■ ▪ (harmful, noisy, toxic, wasteful, dirty, damage, compost)
- ■ ▪ ▪ (poisonous, damaging, chemicals, packaging, energy)
- ▪ ■ ▪ (polluted, resources, disposal, recycle)
- ▪ ■ ▪ ▪ (recyclable, renewable, reusable, environment)

14B Decisions

Action

- ■ **Read and write minutes**
- ■ **Listen to meetings**
- ■ **Make recommendations**
- ■ **Grammar: future perfect**

Speaking: minutes of a meeting

1 To introduce the topic, ask learners these questions: *What kind of meetings do you go to? Are they useful? Why / why not? How are they organised?* Check learners understand *chairperson.* Then they discuss the questions in pairs and as a class. Find out if any of the learners have taken minutes and what the experience was like.

Key

1 suggested answers
  a They are a formal record of what happened at a meeting. They show all the decisions that were made.
  b The date of the meeting, the people who were / weren't present, decisions that were made, action points.

Listening to a meeting

2 Learners listen to the tape and answer the two questions. Check answers.

🔊 *(A = Anne   P = Peter   L = Len   C = Carol)*
  A: *Right, let's start then. Maggie Price sends her apologies – she's in a meeting with a client. You know Carol Pearson, my secretary, don't you?*
  P: *Yes, of course.*
  L: *Hello, Carol.*
  A: *Carol's kindly agreed to take minutes of our meetings. So, the first point on the agenda concerns the appointment of an environmental consultant. The board's agreed that we need outside help from a specialist to look at our work practices and suggest improvements. So we need to approach a suitable person or organisation. Len, I think you've been taking care of that?*
  L: *Yes, there are four local organisations that could help. Er ... they're called Business Care, Green Alert, Efficient Living and Our Earth. I've spoken briefly to all of them and Green Alert seems by far the most professional. Their fees seem reasonable too, so I suggest we start by speaking to them in a bit more depth.*
  P: *I know Mary Hill, who works there, quite well.*
  A: *OK, well why don't we ask Mary Hill to our next meeting. Peter, will you contact her?*
  P: *Yes, fine.*
  A: *But we should make it clear that it's only to talk about her possible involvement in helping us set environmental goals – no commitment. OK, let's move on. Point two ... keeping colleagues informed about what we're doing. Very important if we want them to feel part of the changes that are going to be made.*
  L: *And we should have some way of asking them for their opinions and ideas too.*
  A: *Yes, of course. Now, how shall we do that?*
  L: *Well, we could copy the minutes of these meetings to them.*

A: *Well, the directors certainly want copies. Carol, can you arrange that?*

C: *Yes, right.*

P: *Why don't we do a chatty news-sheet for everyone else? We could use it to make people aware about environmental issues as well as what we're doing in this group. I haven't got a lot of time myself, though.*

A: *Well, I'd be happy to do it, with Carol's help … if the directors agree that I can do it in company time. We'll need some money for it too. I'll bring a sample news-sheet to our next meeting if they approve. And I'll have calculated the cost by next Wednesday's directors' meeting. So let's go on to our last point … finances. Len, you were going to talk to John and Penny.*

L: *Yes, I did. They really want Vision Design to be seen as a green company, so they know that there'll be costs involved in an environmental policy – including the cost of staff time. They do want to know what those costs are likely to be before we start spending anything, though, and of course they will hire the consultant themselves after we make a proposal to them.*

A: *Fine, right, well we need to meet this Mary Hill first. So let's just agree on future meetings. Is everyone happy with Tuesdays?*

P: *Hmm. They're difficult for me. Would Thursday be possible? 4.30?*

L: *No problem for me.*

A: *Yes, that's fine. Shall we make it the second Thursday in each month?*

L: *Fine.*

P: *Yes, good.*

A: *So the next meeting's on January 14th. Right. Oh, well, thanks for coming.*

Key

2a The appointment of an environmental consultant; communication of the Environmental Group's work to other members of staff; financial support for the environmental policy; dates of future meetings.

b Peter will invite Mary Hill from Green Alert to the next meeting. Carol will copy the minutes of their meetings to the company directors. Anne and Carol will produce a sample news-sheet for next meeting. Anne will calculate the cost of a news-sheet.

c After they meet Mary Hill, they will make a proposal for financial support to the directors.

d They will meet on the second Thursday of each month.

Reading minutes

3 a Learners read the minutes and discuss the questions. Check that learners understand *headings*.

b Learners discuss the question in pairs and as a class.

Key

3a C because they contain all the important information clearly, briefly and accurately.

b Good minutes: are clear, brief and correct; are organised under headings, following the points on the agenda; include a record of people attending; contain action points.

Grammar: future perfect

Use the tape to elicit what Anne says about calculating the cost. Write her sentence on the board.

4 Learners discuss the exercise. Highlight the form on the board. Drill the sentence for the correct pronunciation of *I'll have* /aɪləv/.

5 Copy the names onto the board. Refer learners to the action points in minutes C. Learners do the exercise in pairs. Write their answers on the board.

6 Copy these sentence beginnings onto the board:
- **Since last week, I …**
- **By the end of this week, I'll …**
- **By the end of this week, I won't …**

Complete the sentences about yourself and tell the class. In pairs, learners do the same. Make sure they make notes about their partner. They use their notes to report what their partner said to the class. Correct any errors you heard.

Key

4a No, she doesn't. **b** Yes, she will. **c** No, we don't.
d *will have* + past participle

5a Peter will have asked Mary Hill to attend the Group's next meeting.

b Anne will have calculated the cost of producing a news-sheet. Anne and Carol will have produced a sample news-sheet.

c Carol will have produced minutes and copied them to the directors.

Extra practice

P **14.1** Photocopy the questionnaire on page 85. Learners add two more things that they want to ask. Learners mingle and interview each other. They write the learners' names in the appropriate box and then report their findings to the class, e.g. *Angelo will have spent a lot of money. Olga won't have spent a lot of money.*

Listening and Writing: minutes

7 a Play the tape once for learners to note down the main headings. Check answers.

b Learners listen again and make notes.

c In pairs, they compare answers. Then they write the minutes. For feedback, they read each others' minutes and decide which are the best using the criteria in Exercise 3b.

(S = Sam   J = John   P = Penny)

S: *Right, let's start. Patrick will be taking the minutes as usual. Now, I asked Anne Byron to join us, but she's been called away suddenly on a personal matter. Let's see, yes, the first item of business is new staff. How is Pam doing, John?*

J: *I'm a bit worried about her, actually, Sam. She's got a real problem with punctuality – she was nearly an hour late yesterday. I've spoken to her, but we'll have to see.*

S: *Hmm. And you've been interviewing for a new secretary, Penny?*

P: *Yes, I'll have seen everyone by the end of this week, so I'll bring the files of the best three to next week's meeting and we can make a decision.*

S: *Anything else on new staff? No? Good. Let's move on, then. Environmental policy. Anne has left me some notes …*

yes. *As you know from their minutes, the Environmental Group met on December 8th, and they have now contacted Mary Hill. She's agreed to attend their next meeting, and then we'll decide whether to hire her. We'll wait for the group's proposal before we discuss finances, but Anne has asked for £1,500 a year to produce a news-sheet for all staff. It will also take four hours of her time each month and a day of Carol's time. Any comments?*

P: *No, I think that sounds reasonable.*

J: *Yes, why don't we agree to that for six months initially, and review it at the end of that period.*

S: *Agreed. Then there's only one more important issue this week, which you raised, Penny, and that's parking.*

P: *Yes, the car park is so crowded now that clients can't park there – and of course there's no parking on the street outside. I've done an informal survey, and about 80% of our staff come to work in their own car ...*

J: *... which is ridiculous, when we're so near the station and there's a bus stop on the corner. Some of them should share cars – as Penny and I do. This might be a good subject for Anne's first news-sheet. She could explain the problem for clients and for the environment. Then she could suggest alternatives to using cars.*

S: *An excellent idea. Will you speak to her, then, John?*

J: *Certainly.*

S: *Right. Anything else?*

P: *Oh, can we start the meeting slightly later next week? I've got to be in London and I won't be back until three.*

S: *That's fine with me – three thirty, then? John?*

J: *Fine.*

S: *OK. Let's close this meeting, then. Are you playing tennis this evening, Penny?*

Key

7   suggested answer

VISION DESIGN LTD

Minutes of the directors' meeting held on ....

Present: Sam Tenby (ST), John Lane (JL), Penny Wright (PW)

Minutes: Patrick

Apologies: Anne Byron

1 New staff: Pam has a punctuality problem. JL is monitoring the situation. PW is interviewing for a new secretary and will bring files on the best three to the next meeting for a decision. ACTION: JL, PW.

2 Environmental policy: The Environment Group have invited a consultant, Mary Hill, to their next meeting. The Group will then make a proposal about hiring her. It was agreed that, for a six month trial period, Anne should produce a news-sheet for staff. The cost will be £1,500 a year, she and Carol will work on it in company time. ACTION: AB

3 Car parking: Since the car park is overcrowded, staff should use public transport or share cars. JL will ask Anne to discus the problem in her first news-sheet. ACTION: JL.

4 Next meeting: This will begin at the later time of 3.30pm.

Speaking: making recommendations

Brainstorm expressions learners know for making recommendations. Write them on the board. Then they compare their ideas with the expressions in the Phrasebook. Drill the sentences for correct stress and intonation.

8 Remind learners of the problem that Vision Design have with parking. Ask *What recommendations could you make?*

Elicit ideas and write them on the board. Learners discuss other ideas in pairs and as a class.

Extra practice

P 14.2 Divide learners into **A**s, **B**s and **C**s. Photocopy the rolecards on page 85 and give one to each learner. In their groups of three, the first learner explains their problem – encourage them to use their imagination. The others make recommendations about what they should do. The person who makes the best recommendation gets the card. Compare recommendations at the end of the activity. This activity can also be done at the end of 14C to incorporate the language from the second Phrasebook.

14C In the home

Action

- Talk about waste disposal
- Read about a local campaign
- Discuss proposals
- Vocabulary: projects
- Grammar: *-ing* forms

Speaking: waste disposal

1 a Write the categories in the questionnaire on the board. Demonstrate the task: ask *What can you see in the picture?* Elicit one of the items and write it next to the correct category on the board. In pairs, learners do the same for the other types of waste. Write their answers on the board for the next exercise.

b–e Learners discuss the questions in pairs and as a class.

Key

1a glass: bottles
paper: newspaper, paper bag
vegetable/garden waste: leaves, apple cores, carrots
plastic: (none)
metal: cans, tins
clothing: shoe, vest
other: household waste (food): fish

Reading: a local campaign

2 Learners read the text and make brief notes about the project. In pairs, they summarise what the project is about. Check as a class.

Key

2   The project is a four-year campaign to teach the people of Uppsala about recycling and to encourage them to recycle as much of their waste as possible. They will receive an information pack and labels for their own bins. The Council will provide larger containers and there will be public events to promote the campaign.

Vocabulary: projects

3 Write the expressions on the board. Learners discuss the exercise in pairs. Write the best explanation on the board.

> **Key**
>
> **3** *works to a budget:* keeps the cost of a project within agreed limits.
> *draws up marketing strategies:* plans different ways of promoting a product or service.
> *behaviour and attitudes:* what people do and what they think.
> *a starter pack:* the basic equipment and instructions that you need to start doing something.
> *to raise awareness of individual responsibilities:* to make people think about what they should do because it is the right thing to do.

Grammar: *-ing* forms

4 Copy the three phrases in the exercise onto the board. Discuss the exercise as a class.

5 Learners discuss the exercise. Refer learners back to the expressions on the board from Exercise 4. Establish what part of speech *recycling* is in the other phrases.

6 Learners complete the sentences. Compare answers in pairs and as a class. Establish why *-ing* forms are used in each set of sentences.

> **Key**
>
> **4** the Council is not recycling all the waste (verb)
> **5a** B, D, F **b** C **c** A, E
> **6a** • Composting is making vegetable waste into compost.
> • Recycling is using materials again instead of throwing them away.
> • Polluting means making the environment dirty.
> **d** • a boring lesson • a surprising gift • a tiring journey

Extra practice

Copy these sentence halves onto the board:

1 is good exercise.
2 in asking John – he won't know.
3 a service charge in a restaurant.
4 to hearing from you.
5 going to football matches.
6 applying for a new job.
7 smoking.
8 down the street when I saw them.

Learners work in teams. Read out the first sentence beginning below. The first team to say a suitable ending gets a point. Continue in the same way.

a She's thinking of
b There's no point
c I object to paying
d They were walking
e He's just given up
f They're very keen on
g Walking
h I'm looking forward

Speaking: discussing proposals

Books closed. Copy this onto the board:

Accepting proposals
1 People won't .... composting garden waste.
2 I don't object .... walking to work.
3 It's .... controlling the use of central heating.

Rejecting Proposals
4 It's not worth .... people to give up their cars.
5 There's no point .... forcing people to change their lifestyles.
6 We can't .... losing voters by making demands.

In pairs, learners complete the sentences. If necessary, write the missing words on the board in random order (**risk, in, worth, asking, mind, to**). Books open. Learners look at the Phrasebook to check answers. Highlight the form of the prepositions and *-ing* forms. Drill for correct stress and intonation.

7 a Explain the situation and ask learners to read the list of regulations. They add at least four other proposals to the list.
b In pairs, learners discuss their proposals using the expressions on the board. They decide which ones will work and report their decision to the class. Finally, discuss which ones the learners do / don't do and why.

Grammar backup 14

Future perfect

> **Key**
>
> **1b** When will you have finished writing that urgent report?
> **c** They won't have finished their meeting in an hour's time.
> **d** Everyone will have learned how to use a computer in twenty years' time.
> **2b** She will have typed the minutes.
> **c** She will have drawn up the agenda.
> **d** She might have found the latest proposal.
> **e** She might have calculated the budget.
> **f** She won't have sent out the news-sheet.
> **g** She won't have put together a starter pack.

-ing forms

> **Key**
>
> **1b** Spending **c** visiting **d** to see **e** applying
> **f** giving **g** to go **h** travel
> **2b** Don't worry. They're used to **working** late if they have to.
> **c** If you have to **speak** in a foreign language for a long time, it can be very tiring. / **Speaking** in a foreign language for a long time can be very tiring.
> **d** I can go to the meeting if you're **feeling** ill.
> **e** I really don't like **spending** so much money on a new computer system.
> **f** They enjoy **going** to the cinema at the weekends.
> **g** Three of my colleagues are French-**speaking**.
> **h** I'd like **to propose** a compromise.
> **i** Here's the file **containing** all the papers.

15 The information age

15A Information overload?

Action

- Listen to an interview
- Read a newspaper report
- Talk about information overload
- Vocabulary: suffixes
- Grammar: articles *a, an, the*, no article (Ø)

Listening to an interview

1 Discuss what a graphic designer does and how Jacob Bergström might use the Internet. Check that learners understand *a tool*. Play the tape for learners to compare their ideas. Discuss as a class and find out what they use / would like to use the Internet for.

> *I don't actually work with interactive media at Intra, although I have the skills – I work on the design of print materials like brochures. I do use the Internet a lot, though, and of course I need English for that. I look for well-designed Web sites and study the typefaces and so on – that's a professional interest. Then I shop on the Internet, read about music, and look for particular information. There's a frightening amount of information out there, and like all media you can't believe everything you read, but as far as I'm concerned the Internet's a tool, a quick way of finding something I need.*

Key

1 He looks for well-designed Web sites and studies the typefaces. He also shops on the Internet, reads about music and looks for information.

Reading a newspaper report

2 Learners look at the picture and discuss **a**. Then they discuss the meaning of the expressions in **b**.

3 **a** Learners read the report and check their answers to Exercise 2.
b–d Learners read the report again and answer the questions. Check answers.

Key

2a How computers can take over your life.
b • *the explosion in electronic communications:* the huge increase in the amount of correspondence and information being sent electronically.
 • *information overload:* inability to cope with the amount of information coming in.
 • *information fatigue syndrome:* mental disturbances caused by excess information.
 • *The Information Age:* a name given to the modern electronic era to suggest that we have more information available to us than ever before.
 • *computer rage:* frustration with / anger at technology expressed in physical or verbal violence towards your computer.

3b An impossible situation. Trying to cope with the amount of information coming in is as impossible as trying to climb a ladder up Niagara Falls.
 c You become forgetful, get headaches, are bad tempered, lose concentration, your sleep is disturbed and you are anxious.
 d The excessive amount of data that comes to you.

Vocabulary: suffixes

4 Learners look at the report and complete the chart. Compare answers in pairs. Write their answers on the board. Get learners to use the words in sentences to check concept. Then mark the stress on the board and drill for correct pronunciation. Discuss **b** as a class. Use the chart to highlight their answers. Follow the same procedure for **c** and **d**.

Key

4a, d

VERB	NOUN	ADJECTIVE
explode	**explosion**	explosive
communicate	**communication**	communicative
forget	**forgetfulness**	forgetful
disturb	**disturbance**	**disturbing**
concentrate	**concentration**	**concentrated**

b nouns; adjectives

c, d

VERB	NOUN	ADJECTIVE
persuade	**persuasion**	**persuasive**
operate	**operation**	**operational**
–	**thoughtfulness**	thoughtful
accept	**acceptance**	**accepting**
create	**creation**	creative

Extra practice

Write the verbs in Exercise 4 on the board. Learners work in threes. **A** says the first verb on the board and puts it in an example sentence. **B** then says the noun and gives an example sentence and **C** does the same for the adjective. Then **C** begins with the next verb. If you wish, you can do this as a competitive activity with the learners working in three teams.

Grammar: articles – *a, an, the* and no article (Ø)

5 **a** First learners read the grammar box. Then as a class, discuss the uses of the article in the first sentence. Learners categorise the uses of the articles in the other sentences in the same way. Check answers.
b Learners translate the sentences in **a** into their own language. Compare how they use articles as a class.

6 Learners complete the text. Check answers.

Speaking: information overload

7 Find out if learners have ever experienced anything similar to *information fatigue syndrome*. Brainstorm the ways learners receive information, e.g. direct mailings, roadside advertising etc. Then they discuss the exercise in pairs and as a class.

15B Priorities

Action

■ **Read and prioritise correspondence**
■ **Write responses**
■ **Vocabulary: collocations**

Reading and Speaking: prioritising correspondence

Draw this mindmap on the board:

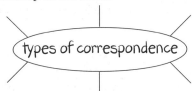

Use it to brainstorm types of correspondence. Compare learners' ideas with the examples on pages 120 and 121. Check learners understand *throw in the bin*. They read the correspondence and answer the questions. Check answers.

Vocabulary: collocations

2 Copy the exercise onto the board. Demonstrate the task: ask *What does Jim confirm in A?* Write the arrangements next to **a** on the board. Learners find the other nouns in the same way. Write their answers on the board. See if learners can think of any other nouns that collocate with the verbs (see Key for ideas).

Extra practice
Learners work in small groups. Read out the first question. Give learners a minute to write down as many answers as possible. Do the same with the other questions. For feedback, each group reads out their answers.
Questions
1 How can you confirm an appointment?
2 Where can you hold a conference?
3 How long do you usually have to pay an invoice?
4 What can you win?
5 What do you do if you want to apply for a new passport?
6 What do you do if you need to see several people at the same time?

Writing responses

3 First learners decide which pieces of correspondence need a response. Then they write the response. They can do this in pairs, or half the class replies to D and the other half replies to H. They swap writing and correct any factual or language errors. This exercise can also be done for homework.

H
FAX
To: Sarah Smith, Mailfast
From: Kathy Elliott, Portman Computer Accessories
Date: May 28th
Re: Meeting
Pages: 1 (including this one)

Ms Spender has asked me to arrange a meeting with Mr Patrick Jones, here at our offices, for some time next week. Here are the times when Ms Spender is free. Could you please let me know which time is most convenient for Mr Jones?
Tuesday 29th – afternoon (from 3 p.m.)
Thursday 1st – morning (between 10 a.m. and midday)
Friday 2nd – afternoon (2–3 p.m.)
I look forward to hearing from you.
Yours sincerely
Kathy Elliott

15C E-mail

Action

- Talk about electronic mail
- Read and write e-mail messages
- End e-mail messages

Reading e-mail messages

1 Find out if learners use e-mail, what for, how often etc. Learners look at the information on the computer screen and answer **a–c**. Check answers. Discuss **d** as a class. If any of them have an e-mail address, ask them to say it to the class. The other learners write it down. To check that they have written the correct address, elicit it from the learners and write it on the board.

2 Learners read messages 1 and 2 and answer **a** and **b**. Check answers and discuss **c** as a class.

3 Copy the three headings in the exercise onto the board. Learners read messages 1–3 and write the expressions next to the three headings. Write their answers on the board. Leave them there for the next exercise.

4 Learners read message 4 and discuss the exercise. Write the message ending from message 2 on the board. Elicit other endings that learners know and write them on the board. They compare their list of endings with those in the Phrasebook. Write any ones that are missing on the board. Find out which ones learners use the most / least. Remind learners of when we use *Yours sincerely* and *Yours faithfully*.

Key

1a 3   **b** Leif at Intra   **c** Intra information
    d flo at perry dot u k, tim smith at superpic dot co dot u k
2a snales@compuserve.com
    b 1 To confirm that Leif is sending the information and the time it should arrive.
    2 To confirm that the information has arrived and to ask for additional information.
    c He'll probably press *delete* because there's nothing he needs to keep in the message. *In-basket* means he'll store it to read later. *File it* means it will go into a filing system. *Reply* will call up an empty e-mail frame for him to write a reply. *Forward* allows him to send the e-mail on to someone else if he wishes. *Cancel* will take the message off the screen but it will remain listed as an incoming message to be read, until he deletes it.
3a Hi! Good morning.
    b We'll, You'll, photos, info, you've, EU, US, Also need to know.
    c Best regards. All the best.
4a No. The people do not know each other. It is a standard, formal reply from a hotel.
    b Yours sincerely.
    c Not really. Formal e-mails and formal faxes contain very similar language. E-mails also include e-mail addresses.

Writing e-mail messages

5 Learners write e-mail messages for the two situations. If possible, they write them on a computer and print them out. Encourage them to swap messages to check for factual and stylistic errors. This exercise can be done for homework.

Key

5a From: Leif Nordlund, INTERNET:leif@intra.se
    To: Andy Snales, snales@compuserve.com
    Date: 29/5/98 10.05
    Re: Intra information
    Hi again! We've got the additional information you asked for, but there's too much to e-mail or fax. My secretary will put it all in the post to you tomorrow.
    Bye for now. Leif leif@intra.se
    b To: Mr Alan Janiurek, janiurek@bignet.com
    From: Hotel des Beaux Arts, beauxarts@franconet.com
    Date: 28/5/98 09.14
    Re: Reservation / June 21–22
    Thank you for your enquiry. We do have a double room available for the nights of June 21–22, but I'm afraid we do not have any 'no smoking' rooms. The hotel has a free car park. The rate for the room is 600 francs excluding breakfast.
    If you would like to make a reservation, please contact us with your credit card number. We look forward to hearing from you.
    Yours sincerely
    J Dumas, Manager
    beauxarts@franconet.com

Extra practice

 P 15.1 Photocopy the worksheet on page 86. Learners work in pairs. If possible, organise them to sit back to back. **A** dictates their e-mail to **B** who writes it down. Then **B** dictates their letter to **A**. To check answers, they compare their writing with the original texts to see how similar they are.

Grammar backup 15

Articles a, an, the, no article (Ø)

> **Key**
>
> **1** **The** way we communicate has changed dramatically over **the** past ten years. More and more people are beginning to use (Ø) e-mail in their working lives and (Ø) voice mail has been introduced into many offices as a way of helping people to communicate. And outside (Ø) work, (Ø) life has changed dramatically as well. (Ø) Most people now own **an** answer machine and many carry (Ø) mobile phones. However, this is not always popular with the people around them: for example, in the UK, some railway companies have introduced carriages where no phones or laptop computers are allowed so passengers can enjoy **a** peaceful journey.
>
> **2b** a   **c** the   **d** the   **e** a, the   **f** an   **g** (Ø)

Sound check

Intonation

Emphasising what's important

1 **a** Copy the sentences onto the board. Learners discuss **a** in pairs and as a class. Do not confirm their ideas yet.
b Play the tape for them to check their answers. Discuss why the words are stressed and establish that the stress depends on the context and how the speaker feels.
c Learners practise saying the sentences.

> *Shall we get them a T-shirt each?*
> *John would like a T-shirt but I think Kate would prefer some chocolates.*
> *Oh, that's absolutely wonderful!*
> *Well I would prefer to go home now.*

2 Learners practise the conversation in pairs. Make sure they change roles. Then play the tape for them to check their sentence stress.

> A: *Can I help you?*
> B: *Yes. Do you sell children's clothes?*
> A: *No, I'm afraid we only sell clothes for adults.*

> **Key**
>
> **1a** T-shirt, John, Kate, chocolates; wonderful; now
> **b** The words are stressed because the speaker is selecting them as being important. *T-shirt* is stressed the first time it occurs because it is new information. *John* is stressed because the speaker is contrasting him with *Kate*. *T-shirt* is NOT stressed the second time because it's not presented as new information. *Kate* is stressed because she is contrasted with *John*. *Chocolate* is new information and is therefore stressed. *Now* is stressed because the speaker is impatient / bored.

Rising and falling intonation

1 **a** Write **The factory's near Moscow ...** on the board three times. Get learners to read **a**, then play the tape. Check answers.
b Learners discuss **b**. Mark the intonation patterns on the board.

> *The factory's near Moscow.*
> *The factory's near Moscow?*
> *The factory's near Moscow ...*

2 Copy the conversation onto the board. Learners listen and complete the gaps at the end of the sentences with the correct intonation pattern. Compare answers in pairs. Then mark the intonation on the board. Books closed. In pairs, learners take it in turns to practise the conversation. As they practise, erase parts of the conversation on the board until they are practising it from memory.

> A: *I'm going to visit that company in Paris.*
> B: *You are?*
> A: *The boss wants me to collect some things ...*
> B: *Things?*
> A: *You know, some brochures, a few samples and he wants a price list.*

> **Key**
>
> **1a** and **b** B is a question. Rising intonation often suggests a question.
> A is a complete statement. Fall-rise intonation often suggests that the speaker intends to continue.
> C is an incomplete statement. Falling intonation often suggests that the speaker has finished speaking.
> **2** A: I'm going to visit that company in Paris (↘)
> B: You are (↗)
> A: The boss wants me to collect some things (↘)
> B: Things (↗)
> A: You know, some brochures (↗), a few samples (↗) and he wants a price list (↘).

Under pressure

16A The ideal secretary

Action

- **Talk about secretarial tasks and qualities**
- **Read a survey extract**
- **Listen to a secretary**
- **Discuss doing personal tasks**
- **Vocabulary: secretarial tasks and qualities**

Speaking: secretarial tasks and qualities

1 Learners look at the cartoon and discuss the exercise.

2 Learners discuss the exercise in pairs and as a class. Write their answers to **e** on the board. Leave them there for Exercise 4.

Key

1a HE'SINAMEETING PLC.
 b Because he is very pleased with himself.
 c A big problem is going to happen.
2c Speaking on four telephones at the same time, feeding a client, word processing.

Vocabulary: the ideal secretary

3 Copy **a** onto the board. Learners find the expression in the survey and decide which answer is correct. Cross out the wrong one. Learners do the same for the other words. Check answers. Drill the words for correct stress.

Key

3b make (a difficult situation) better
 c mail coming into the office
 d answered by a secretary
 e ability to do things correctly
 f ability to keep information private
 g a method of notetaking

Reading: a survey extract

4 Check learners understand *junk mail*. Refer learners back to their lists on the board from Exercise 2. They read the survey extract and compare their answers. Check their answers and discuss **b**.

Key

4a tasks: screen phone calls, make excuses, open most incoming mail, keep a diary, arrange meetings and travel, prioritise visitors, understand the boss's business, computing / word-processing skills, personal tasks, shorthand.
 qualities: common sense, an excellent memory, the ability to defuse difficult situations, flexibility, good interpersonal skills, efficiency, accuracy, initiative, confidentiality, the ability to work in a team, foreign language knowledge. (Note: some of these skills and qualities are only considered important by a small percentage of employers in the survey.)

Extra practice

Learners conduct their own survey. Outside the lesson, they interview 20 or more people using the same survey. Then in class, they report their findings and compare them with those in Exercise 4.

Listening and Speaking: personal tasks

5 Learners listen to the tape and answer the questions. Check answers.

There are some things I won't do because I just think they're insulting. I won't clean the office and it's not my job to keep the plants alive. I'm not a cleaner and I'm not a servant – I'm a secretary and personal assistant. I'll make coffee for my boss sometimes, but he also makes coffee for me. Well, that's fine. But I don't want him to think he can treat me like a servant. In general I'll do anything that's important for the company's business. I'll look after the clients in the day, and sometimes I'll take them out to dinner in the evening. I'll even go shopping to buy gifts for clients, but I won't do any personal shopping for my boss. When my boss asks me to do anything, I always think – would he ask me to do this if I were a man. If the answer's yes then I'll probably do it.

6 Learners discuss the exercise in pairs. They report their decisions to the class.

Key

5a • will: make coffee, do anything that is important for the company's business, look after clients and take them out to dinner, buy gifts for clients.
 • won't: clean the office, look after the plants, do personal shopping for the boss.
 b She refuses to do certain tasks because they are insulting. She is not a cleaner or a servant.

16B Customer service

Speaking: customer services

1 Learners discuss the exercise in pairs and as a class.

Key

1 The main function of Customer Services Departments is to give customers or clients advice and to help with their problems. People usually contact them when they have a problem with a product or service, or when they want to make a complaint.

Vocabulary: qualities and attitudes

Books closed. Copy these words and chart onto the board:

**attentive   interested   organised   sincere
friendly   professional   helpful   pleasant
welcoming**

in	un	dis	well-

Learners write the words in the correct column according to the prefix they can take. As you check answers, ask learners to give example sentences. Establish the difference between *uninterested* (not interested) and *disinterested* (to be fair, not to take sides).

2 Learners discuss the exercise in pairs or as a class. Drill the adjectives for correct pronunciation.

Key

2a Picture 4. The assistant looks well-organised and efficient, friendly and welcoming.

b and c Picture 1: the assistant looks disorganised, inefficient and unprofessional.
Picture 2: the assistant looks efficient but unwelcoming.
Picture 3: the assistant looks hostile, defensive and unhelpful.

Extra practice

Learners work in small groups. You say the words in the exercise, learners say an opposite adjective, e.g. You: *hostile*, Learners: *welcoming*. The first group to say the correct opposite gets a point. You can also use these adjectives: *expensive, travelled, confident, sociable, accurate, sympathetic, educated, capable, reliable, insensitive, fashionable, enthusiastic, diplomatic, desirable, familiar, efficient, flexible, concerned.*

Listening and writing: dealing with difficult customers

3 Learners discuss **a–c** in pairs. Compare their ideas as a class but do not confirm them yet. Play the tape for learners to see if their ideas are the same. Check answers.

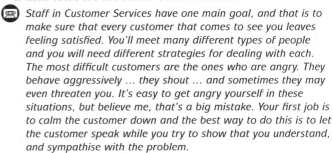

Staff in Customer Services have one main goal, and that is to make sure that every customer that comes to see you leaves feeling satisfied. You'll meet many different types of people and you will need different strategies for dealing with each. The most difficult customers are the ones who are angry. They behave aggressively ... they shout ... and sometimes they may even threaten you. It's easy to get angry yourself in these situations, but believe me, that's a big mistake. Your first job is to calm the customer down and the best way to do this is to let the customer speak while you try to show that you understand, and sympathise with the problem.
The second group of customers I want to mention are those who are confused. Many customers find it difficult to explain their problem. This might be because they don't understand something – about a product ... or about payment, or something like that; it might be because they're elderly ... or perhaps they're just nervous. It's surprising how nervous some people can be in these situations. Whatever the reason, some people find it difficult to be clear about what exactly is wrong and how you can help. With people like this the important thing is to ask questions to clarify the problem ... and to guide the customer into explaining what they want. It's important to spend time with this kind of customer.
Then there are those who I call the 'talkers' – the ones who just seem to have come for a conversation and have all the time in the world. They have some reason for being there, but they're more interested in chatting to you endlessly. The best strategy with this kind of customer is to be polite but firm in dealing with the problem and to move the conversation along and bring it to a close. For example, you might say 'Thank you for your valuable comments. I don't want to take up any more of your time.'
Fortunately, most people who come to Customer Services just want information, and on these occasions all you need to do is answer their questions in a polite, friendly and efficient way.

Key

3a To make sure that every customer leaves feeling satisfied.

b Customers who are angry, customers who are confused, and customers who want to talk.

c With angry customers, we should calm them down; with confused customers, we should ask them questions to make the problem clear; with talkers we should be polite but firm while we deal with the problem and bring the conversation to an end.

Listening: a difficult customer

4 Learners listen to the conversation and answer **a–d**. They check answers in pairs and discuss **e–g**. Discuss as a class.

 (C = customer   A = assistant)

C: *Is this where I make a complaint?*
A: *This is Customer Services. Can I help you?*
C: *Are you the manager? I demand to see the manager immediately!*
A: *He's not here at the moment, I'm afraid. Can I help you?*
C: *Look, I've phoned several times already and nothing's happened. I'm not leaving until this is sorted out.*

A: *All right, there's no need to get angry! Just tell me what the problem is.*

C: *Don't you speak to me like that. I've got good reason to be angry and I won't be spoken to in that tone of voice.*

A: *I'm not speaking to you in any tone of voice. I'm just trying to find out what the problem is.*

C: *Well, I'll tell you. I've got a maintenance contract with this company on my computer … a very expensive maintenance contract if you ask me … and it says that if my computer goes wrong, someone will come to my house within 24 hours and repair it.*

A: *Yes …*

C: *Well … four days ago I phoned this place and I spoke to someone and told them I needed an engineer to come and look at it. Nobody came. The next day I called again and you promised me the engineer would call. Nothing. For the next two days I called every half hour, but the phone was engaged all day. It's now four days later and still nothing has happened. Now I've had to drive twenty miles today to find out what's going on. It's unbelievable, the whole thing. I've paid for a contract and when something goes wrong I expect some service. Now what are you going to do?*

A: *I can't believe our lines were engaged all day …*

C: *Are you calling me a liar? How dare you …*

A: *Look, just give me your name and address, will you?*

C: *I can't believe this. You fail to provide a service I've paid for. I come here and all I get is rudeness.*

A: *You're the one who's being rude.*

Key

4a The engineer has not come to repair the customer's computer.

b She is angry, with good reason. Her maintenance contract says that an engineer will come within twenty-four hours and she has now been waiting for four days.

c She is even more angry, with good reason. The assistant has not dealt sympathetically with her complaint.

d He defends the company, does not apologise and is rude to the customer.

e Defensive, unsympathetic and aggressive.

f The customer might walk out.

g The customer will have a very low opinion of the company.

Grammar: *should have (done)*

5 Write the trainer's comments on the board. Ask the class the questions in the exercise to check understanding. Highlight the form and pronunciation of *should have sent / told* on the board. Drill for correct pronunciation.

6 Play the tape again for learners to make notes of what the assistant and customer did wrong. In pairs, they make sentences about what they should and shouldn't have done. Compare ideas as a class.

Key

5a No, they didn't.   **b** No, they didn't.

c No, they didn't.   **d** A past participle.

e To describe a better action than one that was actually done.

6a He shouldn't have been rude to the customer. He should have apologised. He shouldn't have disagreed with the customer. He should have promised to do something immediately.

b She should have spoken more calmly at the beginning. She shouldn't have shouted at the assistant.

Extra practice

P 16.1 Photocopy the worksheet on page 86. Write this conversation framework on the board:

A: **What's the matter? You look miserable.**

B: **I've just ....**

A: **Oh dear, what happened?**

B: **Well, first of all ....**

They use the information on their rolecards to continue the conversation. Encourage them to use their imaginations and to use *should(n't) have (done)* as much as possible. For feedback, learners roleplay their conversations for the whole class.

Speaking: personal experiences

Learners discuss the exercise in pairs or as a class. If they do not have experience of customer services, they can describe people they have met recently in service encounters who have either given a good or bad impression, and say why.

16C Telephone complaints

Action

■ **Talk and read about complaints**

■ **Listen to a complaint and complete a form**

■ **Make and deal with a complaint**

■ **Grammar:** *can't have / must have / might have (done)*

Speaking: complaints

1 Elicit the last time learners complained about something in a service encounter. Learners discuss the exercise in pairs and as a class.

Key

1   **suggested answers**

A clothes shop: poor quality clothes, lack of choice.

A camera manufacturer: faulty goods, delays in production or delivery.

A television company: poor quality programmes, bad language.

An advertising company: offensive advertisements, sexism.

Reading: handling complaints

2 a Demonstrate the task: ask *Which explanation is for sympathise?* Elicit learners' answer. They match the other stages and explanations in the same way. Check answers.
b Each learner decides the order of the stages in **a**. Compare answers in pairs and as a class. Write their suggested order on the board. Do not confirm their answers yet.

Key

2a and b sympathise – d   check – e   listen – a   clarify – b
take responsibility – c   answer / respond – g
sign off – f

Listening to a telephone complaint

3 a Copy the complaint form onto the board. Play the conversation for learners to complete it. Compare answers in pairs and write them on the board.

b Remind learners of the stages on the board from Exercise 2. Play the conversation to '*making me very angry*'. Elicit what stage this is (*listen*). See if this is what learners had as their first stage. Then learners look at the Phrasebook and decide which phrase Sally Oaks uses. Write it on the board next to the first phrase. Do the same for the other stages. Finally, play the tape again. Learners use the tapescript to shadow the conversation.

(S = secretary   C = caller)

s: Good morning, Blackwood Copiers. Can I help you?
c: Hello. I'm phoning to complain about your maintenance service.
s: I see. Can I take your name, please sir?
c: My name? It's Peter England.
s: And the company name, Mr England?
c: I'm phoning from Take Two Limited. I'm the office manager.
s: Take Two. Thank you, Mr England. Right. Could you tell me exactly what the problem is?
c: Yes. We had one of your maintenance men here three days ago to repair a photocopier. He came and had a look at the machine and said it needed a new spare part. He didn't have the part with him but promised to come and fit it the next day. That was three days ago and nothing has happened. We've now been without a copier for nearly a week and it's making my life very difficult ... and making me very angry.
s: I understand how you feel, Mr England. I'm terribly sorry about the delay. I'll do everything I can to sort things out.
c: Well ... look ... I know it's not your fault ...
s: Don't worry, I know delays like this cause a lot of problems. So, the problem is that your photocopier is not working and you need it repaired urgently.
c: Yes. Exactly.
s: Right. Could you give me the repair order details, please, and I'll check on the computer.
c: Yes. The reference number I was given is 40598 and the date your technician was ... er ... it was on Monday ... er ... that was March 5th.
s: OK. Just a moment. I'm just calling it up on the screen. Right. Here it is. Take Two, 26 High Street, Cambridge. Is that right?
c: Yes, that's it.
s: OK. I'm just reading what it says. Right. Yes. I'm afraid the part you needed was out of stock on Monday.

c: Out of stock! It can't have been out of stock! He phoned from my office to check that it was available!
s: I apologise, Mr England. This does seem to be our fault. Somebody here must have made a mistake.
c: I just can't believe it. He phoned from my office, gave them the part number he needed ... oh ... what's the point. Well thank you for the apology, anyway. So what happens now? When am I going to get the copier repaired?
s: Right. I'll see what I can do. The spare part is now in stock and I'll arrange for our technician to come to you immediately. He can be with you in about an hour's time, by about 11 o'clock?
c: Is that definite?
s: Absolutely certain.
c: Well, 11 o'clock would be fine.
s: Good. Let me apologise once again, Mr England. If you have any problems in future, just call and ask for me. My name's Sally Oak and I'm at Customer Services.
c: Right. Thank you for your help.
s: That's all right, Mr England. I'll call you in a few hours to check that the repair has been done.
c: OK. Let me give you a number where you can reach me this morning. Er ... 351782 ... you should get me on that number.
s: 351782. Fine.
c: Thanks again. Goodbye.
s: Goodbye, Mr England.

Key

3a Taken by: Sally Oak
Name of person complaining: Peter England
Position: Office Manager
Company: Take Two Limited
Address: 26 High Street, Cambridge
Telephone number: 351782
Complaint: Photocopier repair not completed from three days ago – spare part not available.
Action promised: Technician to call immediately with spare part (now available).
b Listen: 'Could you tell me exactly what the problem is?'
Sympathise: 'I understand how you feel.'
Check: 'So the problem is ...'
Clarify: 'Could you give me the order details, please?'
Take responsibility: 'I apologise. This does seem to be our fault.'
Answer / respond: 'I'll see what I can do / I'll arrange for ...'
Sign off: 'Let me apologise once again.'

Grammar: *can't have (done), must have (done), might have (done)*

4 Write the two sentences in the exercise on the board. Discuss **a–e**. Follow the same procedure for **f**. Use the board to highlight the form and pronunciation of the contractions. Drill for correct pronunciation.

5 Learners read the diary. Demonstrate the task: read out the example prompt. Get learners to reply using *must have ...* . They do the exercise in pairs. For feedback, pairs roleplay their exchanges for the whole class.

Key

4a Very sure.

b The technician phoned from the office to check that it was available.

c Very sure.

d She has just seen on the computer that the part was out of stock.

e *can't / must* + *have* + past participle

f It is possible that the maintenance man spoke to the wrong person.

5b You can't have visited our Service Department last Friday, Mr Porter. It was a public holiday.

c I can't have ordered the wine for the seventh, Mr Simpson. The office party was on the sixth. I must have ordered it for the sixth.

d You can't have met the Managing Director last Wednesday, Ms Wills. He was in Glasgow.

e You must have spoken to him later in the week, Ms Francis. He only started work here on Tuesday.

f I'm sorry, Mr Jenkins. George might have left the reception unattended for a few minutes.

Extra practice

Write these statements on the board:

1 **The company's profits fell dramatically last year.**
2 **You're in your office and you suddenly hear a loud bang.**
3 **You can't find the figures you need for a meeting.**
4 **Your e-mail system suddenly crashes while you're using it.**
5 **There's no one in the office except you.**
6 **A colleague is looking very pleased.**

Learners work in small groups and make deductions using the language from Exercise 5. Compare ideas as a class.

Speaking: a telephone complaint

6 Divide learners into pairs. They each read the information about their roles. Establish that **B**s must fill in a complaints form and use the expressions in the Phrasebook. They roleplay their conversations. Then they change roles. Get the **A**s to think of something they want to complain about or copy this situation onto the board:

You took your car in for a service three days ago and it still isn't ready, although the service department said that it would only take a day. You need the car for your work and it is very expensive and inconvenient to use trains all the time. Complain about the delay and find out what is happening.

Finally find out if they thought their partner dealt with their complaint well and use the board to correct any errors you heard.

Grammar backup 16

should have (done)

Key

1b should have delivered   **c** shouldn't have been
   d should have been   **e** shouldn't have refused
   f should have phoned / called / rung
2b You ought **to** have come last night. It was a good party.
   c Should I have **asked** them again?
   d I shouldn't **have** lost my temper with my boss.

can't have / must have / might have (done)

Key

1b can't have been.
   c might / may / could have been.
   d must have been.
   e might / may / could have written.
2b He can't have phoned.
   c I might / may / could have ordered some more fax rolls.
   d They can't have read the report (which I sent last week).
   e He might / may / could have caught / missed the plane.
   f All the staff must have gone home.
   g He may / might not have read his e-mail today.

Learning skills

Using dictionaries 1

1 a Check learners know the words. Then they write them in alphabetical order. Compare answers in pairs. Write them on the board. Do not confirm their answers yet.
b Learners use the dictionary extract to check their answers.

2 a Learners read the list of features in the exercise. They look at their dictionaries to see which features it contains. Compare answers in pairs and as a class.
b Learners look at the dictionary extract again and identify which features it contains. Check answers.

3 a Copy the table onto the board. Learners use the dictionary entry to complete the first line. Check answers and complete the table. Do not mark the main stress yet.
b Learners complete the rest of the table. Do not let them use dictionaries at this stage. Compare answers in pairs.
c They use their own dictionary to check their answers to **b**. Complete the table on the board.
d Learners mark the main stress on the words in the table. Check answers. Drill for correct pronunciation.

Key
1b advertisement, advertising, advice, advisable, advise, advisory
2b A, B, C, D, E, F, H, J

3

Noun	Person	Verb	Adjective
ad'vice	ad'visor	ad'vise	ad'visory
a'nalysis	'analyst	'analyse	ana'lytical
appli'cation	'applicant	a'pply	—
represen'tation	repre'sentative	repre'sent	repre'sentative

Using dictionaries 2

1 Learners discuss the exercise in pairs. List their ideas on the board.

2 Copy the words and grammar codes onto the board. Learners discuss **a–c** in pairs and as a class. Highlight their answers on the board.
d Learners compare the codes with the ones in their dictionary. Compare them with their list on the board from Exercise 1.

3 Write these questions on the board:
* **What is teleworking?** (Working from home, using a computer with a modem link to the office.)
* **What are its advantages?** (Fewer cars on the road, more flexible working hours for staff.)
Learners read the newspaper extract and answer the questions. Check answers. Then elicit the words in italics and write them on the board. Learners answer **a** and **b**. Check in pairs. Use the board to collate their answers.

4 Write **firm** and **form** on the board. Elicit what meanings the learners already know for them. Then they use their dictionaries to work out their meanings in the sentences. Compare answers and write them on the board. Find out if they could use two words in their own language for the different meanings.

5 a Learners read the three dictionary entries and answer the two questions. Check as a class.
b Learners find *tell* in their dictionaries. Discuss the exercise in pairs and as a class.

6 Learners use their dictionaries to check the meaning and grammar of the words in the exercise. In pairs, they make up a story using the words. Finally, they read them to the class and decide which story is best.

Key
2a • nouns – age, pay
• verbs – glance, look into
• adjectives – careful
b pay
c look into
3a practice – noun, view – verb, sounds – verb, official – adjective, left – verb (past participle) staff – noun
b **suggested answers**
practice: the action of doing something regularly to get better at it; the place where a doctor works. In American English, *practice* can also be used as a verb. In British English, the verb form is *practise*.
view: noun, an opinion.
sounds: plural form of the noun, things you hear.
official: noun, a person who works in government.
left: adjective, the opposite of *right*, e.g. Turn left out of the office; it's on the left.
staff: verb, to provide the workers for somewhere, e.g. to staff a stand at a conference; the office is staffed by four people.
4a company (noun) **b** strict (adjective) **c** hard (adjective)
d strong (adjective) **e** document for information (noun)
f created (past participle) **g** kind (noun) **h** class (noun)
5a scarf: noun; sink: verb; far: adverb
The entries tell you the singular and plural forms of the noun; the infinitive, past simple and past participle of the verb; and additional spellings and variants of the adverb.

Learning new words

Use this worksheet after learners have studied Unit 1. All the words come from that unit.

1 Learners discuss the exercise in pairs or as a class. If you wish, list the key points on the board.

2 a Learners listen to Friederike and make notes. Check answers.
b Discuss as a class.

(T = teacher   F = Friederike)

T: *So, Friederike, how do you go about learning new words?*

F: *Well, I use this system that I learnt from a colleague at work. We were talking about how we learn vocabulary, he's taking French classes at the moment, and he told me about this really interesting technique that he'd been taught at school.*

T: *How does it work?*

F: *Um, it's all based on cards.*

T: *Cards?*

F: *Yes, cards. You see, during a lesson or when I'm reading something like a book or newspaper, I write down 10 words which I think are really important or useful.*

T: *Or that you like?*

F: *Yes, or that I like. Then, next, I check what they mean in my dictionary and if I still think they're useful …*

T: *Or that you still like them?*

F: *Yes! Then I write them on separate pieces of paper, with the word on one side and the definition and an example sentence on the other.*

T: *For example?*

F: *Well, say I've found the word 'annoying'.*

T: *Yes …*

F: *Right. I write 'annoying' on one side of the card and then its meaning, for example, 'another word for irritating' on the other side with a sentence. So, for example, 'I find it very annoying when people smoke in my house because I hate cigarette smoke.'*

T: *Right, I see now.*

F: *And then I carry the cards around with me in my bag and test myself when I'm on the bus, wherever. Sometimes I put them on the fridge door in the kitchen!*

T: *So that you always see them.*

F: *Yes. Then when I think I know them, I write them in other example sentences or try to use them in class. Then I put them in a box. When I've got 100 words in the box, I test myself again and throw away the ones I can remember. It's very satisfying!*

3 Learners look at the seven techniques and discuss how the words are organised. If you wish, write the techniques on the board. Find out which ones they already use, would like to try to use, or would never use, and why.

4 Learners do the exercise in pairs. If you wish, they can choose the same unit, discuss the exercise and compare their ideas.

5 Discuss the exercise as a class. If you wish, learners work in pairs and use some of the techniques to organise the vocabulary for the Word file they chose in Exercise 4.

Key

1 To know a word means that you: recognise it when you hear / see it; understand when we use it; can say and write it accurately; know its grammar; know what words it goes with; know if it's formal or informal, American or British English; can remember it when you want to.

2a • She writes down 10 words that she finds when reading which she thinks are useful or that she likes.
- She checks their meaning in her dictionary.
- She writes each word on separate pieces of paper, with the word on one side and the definition and an example sentence on the other.

- She carries the cards around with her and uses them to test herself. Sometimes she puts them on her fridge door in the kitchen.
- She writes them in other example sentences or uses them in class.
- She puts them in a box.
- When she's got 100 words in the box, she tests herself again. She throws away the ones she can remember.

3a Pictures to show a topic.

b Words recorded onto a tape recorder.

c Phrases organised in topics with an explanation for each phrase.

d Adjective / noun wordbuilding.

e Words which begin with the same letter, translated from English into the learner's own language.

f A mindmap / spidergram of words for one topic.

g Noun / adjective + noun collocation, words that go together.

Improving your English outside the classroom

1 Books closed. Learners discuss the exercise in small groups and as a class. List the different things they do on the board.

2 Books open. Learners look at the pictures and discuss which ones they do, how often and how it helps their English. Demonstrate the task: read out the idea in **a**. Elicit the reason for doing this. Learners then do the same for the other ideas. Compare answers in pairs and as a class. Discuss which ones they do.

3 Remind learners of their list on the board from Exercise 1. In pairs, they write down one more activity for each area. Discuss as a class and write any new ideas on the board.

4 Learners copy the study plan into their notebooks. They complete it with the two things they are going to do.

Key

2b reading   **c** writing   **d** speaking
e grammar / vocabulary   **f** vocabulary   **g** writing
h listening   **i** grammar   **j** speaking
k reading   **l** speaking (and listening)

3 *Listening:* Watch the news on TV every day.
Reading: Subscribe to an English magazine.
Speaking: Talk to foreigners.
Writing: Get an e-mail pen friend.
Grammar: Use computer games.
Vocabulary: Look up new words in your dictionary.

P 1.1

mail	order	security	check
traveller's	cheque	address	book
city	centre	departure	lounge
tourist	office	exchange	bureau
arrivals	board	newspaper	stand

P 2.1

1 .... and .... have visited four different countries.

2 .... didn't go on holiday last year.

3 .... and .... have got interesting jobs.

4 .... should give up smoking.

5 .... can speak more than two languages.

6 .... has a fast car.

7 .... likes travelling by plane.

8 .... is going to the cinema at the weekend.

9 .... and .... are good at sport.

10 .... will get a promotion next year.

P 2.2

A

B

P 3.1

When Manuel woke up, it .... (still rain) outside and it was dark.
He quickly .... (dress) and .... (leave) for the office.
He knew that he had to get there early if he wanted to do any work before his colleagues .... (arrive). They .... (always / talk) and .... (ask) him questions – it was impossible to get any peace.
But when he got to the office, he had a surprise.
All the lights were on and everybody was already at their desks. No one .... (talk), they .... (work) at their computer terminals.
And when he .... (walk) into the office, nobody stopped typing, they just said 'Hi!'. Manuel .... (look) at the clock on the wall: it was only seven o'clock. He couldn't understand it – what .... (happen)?
Then somebody .... (laugh) and all the staff joined in.
'What's so funny?' Manuel asked.
'April fool!' they all shouted.
And then he .... (look) at the calendar next to the clock and saw it was the first of April!

P 4.1

The beginning
Claudia Moor goes to school in Oxford. She is fifteen and has to choose her A Level subjects. She wants to study French, German and English but her parents think she should concentrate on sciences.
1 *What will happen if she chooses the arts A Levels?*
2 *What might happen if she chooses the science subjects?*
3 *What do you think she'll decide to do?*

Part 2
Claudia chooses to study sciences because she has decided to leave school the day she is sixteen. She does this. Her parents and teachers are very angry.
1 *What will she do next?*
2 *What will her parents do?*

Part 3
Claudia does different temporary jobs in Oxford for a year until she has saved enough money to travel abroad. She gets a job in a hotel in Switzerland for a year.
1 *What will happen to Claudia in that time?*
2 *What will she do after her year there?*

Part 4
Claudia grows up a lot in the time that she works in the hotel. She meets a lot of young people from different countries and begins to learn more about life. She also meets a friend who tells her about a project to build a nature reserve in the south of France. At the same time, she is offered a job in the hotel in charge of the business centre.
What will she do next?

Part 5
Claudia leaves Switzerland and moves to France. While she's working on the project, she meets Pierre and they start going out. But after eighteen months, Pierre leaves for Canada. Claudia is heart-broken.
What will Claudia do next?

Part 6
Claudia is now almost twenty. She decides that she must return to Oxford to get some kind of professional training. She gets a job in a hospital working as an ancillary helper but finds it very difficult to settle down again after two and a half years away. She considers applying to do nursing but her parents think she should go back to college to study for her A Levels.
1 *Will she stay in Oxford or go away again?*
2 *If she stays, what will she study?*

The end
Claudia starts to study nursing at a hospital in London but changes to study social work after a year. She is now the head of social services for Oxfordshire.

P 5.1

Find someone who . . .

.... didn't go out last weekend.

.... is learning a new skill at the moment.

.... hasn't worked on a stand in an exhibition.

.... isn't going on holiday soon.

.... was having breakfast at 9 o'clock this morning.

.... went to a food demonstration or tasting last year.

.... doesn't ask for discounts in shops.

.... has negotiated an agreement with a customer.

.... wasn't watching TV at 7 o'clock last night.

.... works for a company which sponsors events.

P 5.2

1 Take a stand at an international trade exhibition in Paris. £5,000

2 Advertise in the international press. Include a tear-off reply slip for a free sample. £20,000

3 Send a mailshot to all existing customers with information about the *Crispette.* Offer a free sample. £6,000

4 Give out free samples in large supermarkets in the UK. £10,000

5 Organise a wine tasting with free samples of the *Crispette* at famous department stores in London, Paris and New York. £18,000

6 Organise a launch of the *Crispette* at the National Gallery in London. Invite a famous person to open the event. £10,000

7 Offer a two for the price of one discount to customers. £10,000

8 Sponsor a fun-run for charity. £5,000

9 Advertise the *Crispette* in a TV commercial. £30,000

10 Your idea: .... £..........

P 6.1

A → across ↓ down

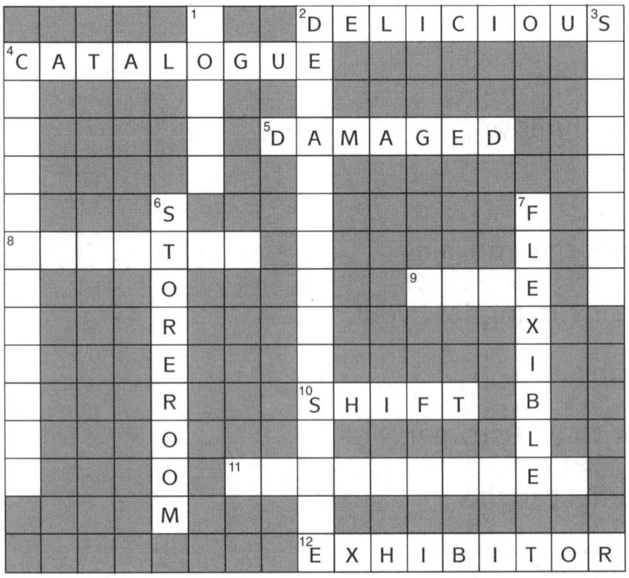

Crossword grid A (filled letters):
- 2 across: DELICIOUS
- 4 across: CATALOGUE
- 5 across: DAMAGED
- 6 down: STOREROOM
- 7 down: FLEXIBLE
- 10 across: SHIFT
- 12 across: EXHIBITOR

B → across ↓ down

Crossword grid B (filled letters):
- 1 down: L
- 2 down: DEPARTMENT
- 3 down: SHOWCASE
- 4 down: CONFECTIONER
- 5 down: A
- 8 across: COUNTER
- 9 across: FAKE
- 10 down: ST R
- 11 across: WHOLESALER
- 12: E

P 7.1

A

B

First the pizza bases (a) .... onto trays. Then the tomato sauce (b) .... After the sauce (c) .... onto the pizza bases, they (d) .... with cheese and olives. The pizzas (e) .... into squares. After they (f) ...., they (g) .... into boxes. Finally they (h) .... to a pizzeria where they (i) .... and served to customers.

P 7.2

a .... is that you can lose your job.

b .... is that you may be stopped by the police.

c .... is not to be interrupted when you're working.

d .... is to have a rest and relax.

e .... is that I'm too tired to concentrate.

f .... was that he was so bored in his old one.

P 8.1

to deliver	to contact	a client	an inquiry
to despatch	to fax	a query	fittings
to discuss	a problem	personnel	to transport
to ship	a buyer	a network	to handle
to damage	to design	to advertise	to print
a reputation	install	a share	a licence
trainee	trainer	interviewee	interviewer
franchiser	employer	employee	franchisee
to greet	to keep	an appointment	to put through
a visitor	to receive	a diary	courier packages

P 9.1

Message 1: This is Susan. I'm going to be late into work. I've cancelled my 9 o'clock meeting with James but I'll need all the papers for the meeting with Anna and Stefan at 11. Can you find them?

Message 2: This is Rebecca. Can you send me the slogans by courier? We need them for the publicity brochure.

Message 3: It's Gabrielle. Don't worry. I'll tell the painters to start tomorrow.

P 10.1

take	on	go	ahead
put	together	set	up
find	out	talk	over
carry	out	put	forward
try	out	tune	in
turn	off	look	forward to

P **11.1**

	Véronique	**David**
Where / live now?		
How long / there?		
Where / live before?		
How long / there?		
Why / saving?		
How much / save / this year?		
How much / save last year?		
How much / the year before?		
How long / saving?		
How much / save / up to now?		

A

12th October

Dear Sarah,

Just a quick note to tell you my new address. I'm sorry I haven't written before but I've been so busy in the two months since I moved into my new flat.

It's okay but I really want to buy somewhere. However, I still haven't got quite enough money. I'm really fed up with economising all the time – it's been three years now. But I suppose I'm doing quite well, actually. Last year I managed to put by £10,000, which isn't bad, and the year before I saved £5,000 more than that. This year's not so good though because we didn't get a summer bonus, so I've only saved another £5,000.

You must visit soon. Hong Kong is such fun, especially after London. I really enjoyed those three years working there with you but it's good to be out of the UK. Hope you'll be able to make it for the Chinese New Year.

All the best

Véronique

B

12th October

Dear Michael,

I thought I'd drop you a quick line to let you know how things are going.

I really like Hamburg and the job is great. And guess what? I've nearly saved enough money to buy that BMW that I've always wanted! You know I started putting some money by when I moved here two years ago. Well this year I've managed to save £6,000 because I've earned so much more in commission, which is really encouraging. The year before last I managed to save double what I saved last year (only £2,000 – I had so many bills to pay).

Do you think you'll be able to come over for my 30th birthday? It'd be great to see you and you'd love Hamburg – it'll be a real change from Oxford. I know I spent the first 20 years of my life there, but I never want to go back!

See you soon, I hope.

Best wishes

David

P 12.1

Stefan's day started badly last Tuesday when he overslept because he (a) .... his alarm clock. When he woke up at 8 o'clock he realised he (b) .... his 7 o'clock flight to Paris. He phoned the airline and got another seat on the 10 o'clock flight and rushed to the airport. But at the check-in he couldn't find his passport – he (c) .... it on the kitchen table. Fortunately his flatmate was still at home and he brought it to the airport. So Stefan got on the next flight at 11 o'clock. As he settled into his seat, he breathed a large sigh of relief – it was good that he (d) .... the meeting to start at 2 o'clock. But then the pilot announced that Orly airport (e) .... because of a security alert and all flights were being diverted to Lille. It took him five hours to get to Paris! By the time he got there, everyone (f) .... home. He knew they were all going out for dinner but they (g) .... to leave him a note with the address of the restaurant. He checked into his hotel, had dinner and went to bed at nine. What a day!

P 13.1

While many companies now have Web sites,
People eat late in the evening in Spain while
It had been a long meeting but
I like living in London,
Although I left a message on his answer machine
I still can't send an e-mail although
In spite of working late every night this week,
Despite recently getting a pay rise,
In spite of the fact that we have economised,
Despite the fact that I sent a memo to all the departments,
they are only effective if they are updated regularly.
in Sweden they have dinner much earlier.
very useful.
it's expensive, though.
he still arrived for the meeting.
I've been shown how to do it three times.
I still haven't finished the annual report.
he still hasn't got any money!
we still cannot afford to install a new computer system.
no one knew that the company had won a special award.

P 14.1

By this time next year, who . . .

	yes	no	maybe
1 spend a lot of money			
2 go abroad			
3 start a new job			
4 learn a lot of English			
5 move to a different town			
6 buy a new computer			
7 give a presentation			
8			
9			

P 14.2

A: You have a colleague / friend who uses the phone to make a lot of personal calls. This is against company rules and you think your colleague should stop, but don't know how to tell them. What should you do?

B: You have worked for your company for two years and feel that you have done a good job and should get a pay rise. You have tried to speak to your boss but she isn't very interested. What should you do?

C: You have a good job but have been doing it for five years and find it boring. You don't want to leave your present company, but there don't seem to be any opportunities for promotion. What should you do?

P 15.1

A

TO: Jeremy Kingston, INTERNET: j.kingston@demon.uk
FROM: Alicia McMichael, INTERNET: mcmichael@compuserve.com
DATE: 16/11/98   09.56
RE: Order No. 6584

Good morning! Thank you for your e-mail/order. The total price for the XLR Computer system is £2,400. Please confirm that this price is acceptable. Once we have heard from you, we will organise delivery by the end of the week. Looking forward to hearing from you.
Best regards
Alicia

B

Ms T Asenage   Global Travel
Computer Systems UK   14 St John's Avenue
Pioneer House   Leeds LS7 2WP
30–36 East Way
York YO6 9QT   25 November 1998

Dear Ms Asenage
Thank you for sending me your catalogue of computer equipment. As you suggested, I think it would be useful if one of your sales representatives could come to our office to demonstrate the features of your latest palmtop computers.
I would be grateful if you could contact me to organise a date.
Yours sincerely
Louis Russell

Human Resources Manager

P 16.1

A
You have just been to a terrible job interview.
1 I forgot to collect my suit from the cleaner's.
2 I missed the train.
3 I couldn't find their office.
4 I was really tired because I went to bed late last night.
5 I didn't have much to say.

B
You have just lost your temper with your secretary.
1 She has been late for work all week.
2 She didn't tell me that the clients had changed the time of our meeting yesterday. They were waiting when I got to work.
3 I lost the notes for the meeting.
4 I kept on getting phone calls during the meeting.
5 The restaurant for lunch was full – she'd forgotten to book a table.

Test 1 (Units 1–4)

Vocabulary

1 **Use the verbs in the box to complete the sentences.**

confirm despatch forward book source
own recommend run attend train

EXAMPLE: I find it easier to ....handle............ my own
correspondence than getting my secretary to
do it.

1 We will .... your order this
afternoon by special courier so it will reach you in
an hour.

2 I won't be here next week because I'm going to
.... a training course to learn how
to use my new software programme.

3 Can you .... John's latest e-mail to
me so that I can see exactly what he has said?

4 I'd like to .... that we ask our staff
what they think of this new proposal.

5 My family used to .... a chain of
high street shops but they sold them ten years
ago.

6 Does Martin Eastwood still .... the
sales department?

7 We need to .... our staff to use the
new computers.

8 I need to go to Alicante next week. Could you
.... me on the first flight on
Monday morning?

9 Please .... that you have received
the cheque that I sent you last week.

10 Micro Electronics want to .... all
their equipment from us.

MARKS /10

2 **Circle the word which is different from the others.**

EXAMPLE: storeroom (vending machine) workshop
airline office

1 wet climate warm windy

2 fun tasteful awful nice

3 confident sympathetic flexible distressing

4 counter display unit showcase transaction

5 exchange rate cheque coin note

MARKS /5

3 **Match the words in the two columns.**

EXAMPLE: tourist ⟶ office

1 boarding   **a** shop

2 frequent   **b** flight

3 long   **c** point

4 lost   **d** lounge

5 duty-free   **e** flyer

6 charter   **f** hire

7 check-in   **g** pass

8 departure   **h** distance

9 car   **i** desk

10 meeting   **j** luggage

MARKS /5

Grammar and Functions

4 **Circle the correct answer to complete the sentences.**

EXAMPLE: .... did you go for lunch? Mario's.

    a When **b** Who ©Where

1 I'll have to take a taxi to the airport tomorrow ....
the meeting finishes after five o'clock.

    a if **b** when **c** before

2 He .... to the airport when his car broke down.

    a was driving **b** drove **c** were driving

3 If we post the order today, I know you .... it by
tomorrow.

    a might have **b** have **c** will have

4 Who .... this report? It's full of mistakes.

    a did type **b** typed **c** was typing

5 I don't like .... of them.

    a both **b** either **c** neither

6 You .... get a taxi – I can take you home.

    a should **b** must **c** needn't

7 People read the *Financial Times* .... they can get
the latest information about the stock market.

    a so **b** to **c** for

8 She used to smoke, ... she?

    a used **b** didn't **c** usedn't

9 I work .... a management consultant for Braithwaites.

   a on **b** to **c** as

10 You .... speak French and English at work, don't you?

   a never **b** must **c** have to

MARKS	/5

5 Circle the correct answers.

EXAMPLE: You aren't *allow* / *(allowed)* to park here.

1 Would you like *change* / *to change* your travellers' cheques?

2 Are you paying *by* / *in* cash?

3 Have you thought *in* / *of* asking your boss for promotion?

4 I'd prefer *earn* / *to earn* less money and have an interesting job.

5 They *definitely won't* / *won't definitely* be here by 12.00.

MARKS	/5

6 Write the complete dialogues. Add words and correct verb forms asnecessary.

EXAMPLE:

  A: Excuse /. Where / to be / the exchange bureau?

  B: It's / the first floor, face / the escalator.

  A: *Excuse* **me***. Where* **is** *the exchange bureau?*

  B: *It's* **on** *the first floor,* **facing** *the escalator.*

1 A: How about / go to the cinema / Saturday?

  B: Good /.

  A: ....

  B: ....

2 A: I suppose we / move the central display unit.

  B: No, I / no think it / work because it's too big.

  A: ....

  B: ....

3 A: Would you mind / wait in line?

  B: Oh, I'm sorry. I / no realise there was a queue.

  A: ....

  B: ....

4 A: Are there / seats on the next flight to Athens?

  B: Just a moment, Sir. I / check for you.

  A: ....

  B: ....

MARKS	/10

Writing

7 You are Jonathan Fox. You are a sales executive at AB Travel. One of your clients phones when you are at lunch. Read the message that your colleague took. Use the notes to write a fax in reply.

> **While you were out ...** ☎
>
> Urgent: please fax reply
> Marie Claire Picot (Abax Communication) rang.
> Have you confirmed Philip Sykes' flights & accommodation for Seattle, USA?
> How much? When receive invoice?

MARKS	/10

Test 2 (Units 5–8)

Vocabulary

1 **Write the words in the correct category.**

> bitter heart-shaped creamy coat tube fresh pour carton spicy hexagonal barrel ~~tin~~ decorate fill rectangular ~~nutty~~ round jar triangular sack ~~pack~~ fold stale ~~square~~

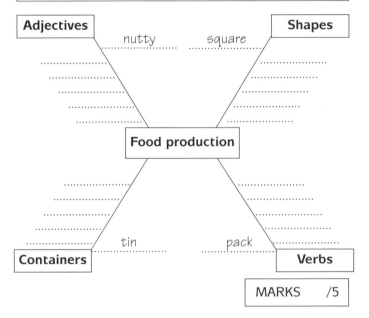

Adjectives
nutty ....

Shapes
square ....

....

....

....

....

Food production

....

....

....

Containers
tin ....

Verbs
pack ....

MARKS   /5

2 **Are these job descriptions correct? If they are correct, tick (✓) them. If they are not, write the name of the correct job.**

EXAMPLE: A client buys products / services from a company. ....✓........

A storeman makes chocolates. ...confectioner...

1 A buyer sells things for a company. ....

2 A packer puts machines together. ....

3 A retailer sells things in shops. ....

4 An exhibitor makes sure that all outlets have the company's goods in stock. ....

5 A buyer gives money towards an event in return for free publicity. ....

MARKS   /5

3 **Read the definitions and complete the adjectives.**

EXAMPLE: exactly correct   ac c u r a t e

1 new and different   in _ _ v _ _ _ _ e

2 another word for *cheap*   i _ e _ _ _ _ _ _ v _

3 difficult to believe   i _ c _ _ d _ _ _ _

4 limited to one person/group   ex _ _ _ s _ _ _

5 separate items   i _ _ _ v _ _ _ _ l

6 very good   f _ _ t _ _ _ _ c

7 nice to look at   pr _ _ _ y

8 very bad   t _ r _ _ b _ _

9 strong, opposite of *weak*   p _ w _ _ f _ _

10 not in perfect condition   d _ m _ g _ _

MARKS   /5

4 **Complete this description of a computer.**

EXAMPLE: Do you need a computer that you can take anywhere? Then the new 3455
..........portable.......... is just the one for you!

KEY FEATURES
The colour (1) .... makes it easy to read text and the well-designed (2) .... makes typing easy! And the built-in (3) .... means that it is unbelievably quick to send faxes and e-mails. With a (4) .... of 2Gb and a 32 Mb memory, it's powerful enough for all your needs. And it has a two-year (5) ....

MARKS   /5

Grammar and Functions

5 **Circle the correct answer to complete the sentences.**

EXAMPLE: This fax isn't as good ...... the others.

 a than   **b** so   **c** as

1 It would be much better if he ...... me the figures the day before our weekly meeting.

 a gives   **b** gave   **c** is giving

2 I listen to people ...... advice is good.

 a who   **b** whose   **c** that

3 I'll test it when all the software ...... installed.

 a are   **b** will be   **c** has been

4 This isn't her first visit. She ...... to Paris several times before.

 a went   **b** has gone   **c** has been

5 We must have the new brochure ...... as soon as possible.

 a printed   **b** print   **c** to print

MARKS   /5

6 Circle the mistake in each sentence and write the correction.

EXAMPLE: I think I (lived) in Algeria when I first met you.
<u>was living</u>

1 The cost of living is higher considerably in Switzerland than in Poland. ....

2 Our sales figures are getting gooder and gooder.

....

3 This fish smells like delicious ....

4 What do you do this evening? ....

5 All our employees can work hardly when they need to. ....

MARKS   /5

7 Look at the graph. Use the words in the box to complete the sentences. Remember to use the correct form of the verb.

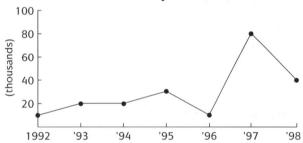

Sales of luxury chocolates

expand	level	~~increase~~	to	fall	rise
dramatically	by	shrink	slightly	remain	

EXAMPLE: 1992–1993: Sales <u>increased</u> .

a 1993–94: Sales .... at the same ....

b 1994–95: Sales ....

c 1995–96: Sales .... 20,000.

d 1996–97: The market ....

e 1997–98: The market .... 40,000.

MARKS   /5

8 Complete the dialogue with the correct expressions.

> What would you like?   What's your name?
> Can I take your coat?   I'll tell him who you are.
> Could I take your name, please?
> Do you want to keep your coat?
> Where are you from?   I had an appointment with
> I'll tell him you're here.   ~~Can I help you?~~
> Which company are you from?
> I've got an appointment with

EXAMPLE: A: Good morning. <u>Can I help you?</u>

B: Good morning. (1) ....
.... Rafael Retmono at 11.

A: (2) ....

B: Yes, it's Rosemary Lucas.

A: And (3) ....

B: Central TV.

A: I see. Just a moment. (4) ....

B: Thank you.

A: (5) ....

B: No thank you. I'm a little cold.

MARKS   /5

Writing

9 Use the information below to write a letter (100–120 words) in reply to the enquiry form.

COMMUNICATIONS *EXPRESS*

How can we help?

Name: Paula Hughes

Address: Office Recruitment, Napier House, 56–59 Edison Street, London WC1 9JK

Information needed: information on all fax and phone machines for office use

Notes

- info on full range of products
- product sheets for Alpha 768 & 945 – new this year. Include all specifications.
- more info? useful to visit office? demonstrate both machines?

Anthony Thompson
Senior Sales Executive

Communications Express
95 The Broadway
London W13 0RT

MARKS   /10

Test 3 (Units 9–12)

Vocabulary

1 Match the verbs with the correct nouns.

verbs	nouns
sum up ———→	a meeting
1 target	**a** work
2 launch	**b** an interview
3 liberate	**c** a machine
4 plot	**d** a town
5 conduct	**e** a rocket
6 drop out of	**f** a body
7 edit	**g** a news item
8 retire from	**h** a graph
9 assemble	**i** the consumers
10 cremate	**j** college

MARKS   /5

2 Complete the chart.

noun	adjective
favour	EXAMPLE: .....favourite.......
enthusiasm	1 ....
sensitivity	2 ....
fashion	3 ....
thought	4 ....
wealth	5 ....

MARKS   /2½

3 Write the words in the correct column.

sitcom   viewer   script   drama   audience
~~voice over~~   soap opera   wire   correspondent
comedy   autocue

TV programmes	people	things which are read
		voice over

MARKS   /2½

4 Use one word from each box to make a phrasal verb to complete the sentences. Do not write in the brackets yet.

draw   talk
tune   go
~~set~~   put

forward   ~~up~~
over   in
ahead   up

EXAMPLE: He wants to ...set up... (.establish.) his own
company when he leaves university.

1 They said we could ....
.... (................................) with the
advertising campaign, but that we could only spend
£10,000.

2 He ....
(................................) his ideas for a new product at
the meeting last week.

3 I think we should ....
.... (................................) the problem
together before the meeting tomorrow.

4 We ....
(................................) to the radio and heard the
news that the prime minister had resigned.

5 He's going to ....
(................................) a questionnaire and give it to
us by the end of the week.

Match each verb below with a phrasal verb in 1–5 with the same meaning. Write your answers in the brackets. Use each verb once.

start   suggest   ~~establish~~   write   listen   discuss

MARKS   /10

Grammar and Functions

5 Circle the correct answer to complete the sentences.

EXAMPLE: Twenty-six-......-old ballet dancer Louise
Watson has been shot in a terrorist attack.

   ⓐ year   **b** years   **c** aged

1 Could you turn on ......? I want to watch the film.

   a television   **b** it   **c** the television

2 Their advertising literature is really well ....

   a written   **b** wrote   **c** write

3 She told us last month that she ...... all the data by the end of next week.

   a will have **b** would have **c** has

4 ...... it's desirable to be multi-lingual in my job, it's not essential.

   a Although **b** Whereas **c** However

5 I always get ...... a bonus in December.

   a to pay **b** pay **c** paid

| MARKS | /5 |

6 There is a word missing from each sentence below. Put the correct word in the correct place, as in the example.

EXAMPLE: I think there are slightly ᵪ *fewer* people at this conference than last year. It's not so busy.

1 Do you know Stephen? He's working for MTV for six months.

2 I always listen to the seven o'clock news. So I!

3 To put another way, I think we should carry out some research.

4 When I started my present job, I never used a database system before.

5 They told me be diplomatic.

| MARKS | /5 |

7 Use the phrases to complete the dialogue.

> can't stand familiar background in
> been working rather ~~work experience~~
> interested like it the best experience of
> prefer capable

EXAMPLE: A: What is your most recent
        work experience?

B: I've got a (1) .... tele-sales with a

  lot of (2) .... working with clients from France and Germany. Altogether, I've

  (3) .... in this field for about fifteen years now.

A: I see. So why do you want a change?

B: Well, I'm very (4) .... in data analysis.

A: Hmm. How good are your computer skills?

B: I'm (5) .... with most word-processing packages although I

  (6) .... Word 6. I must say I

  (7) .... because it's so easy to use.

A: That's fine. So why do you think you would be good at the job?

B: I'm well-organised and am (8) .... of working under pressure. I

  (9) .... not having enough work as I get bored.

A: Is there anything else?

B: If possible, I'd (10) .... not do overtime as I have two small children.

| MARKS | /10 |

Writing

8 You work for Lewis Electronics in the personnel department. You have been asked to write a short report (120–160 words) about how the staff and their conditions of employment have changed since 1980 when the company started. Use the statistics below and your imagination to write your report.

	1980	now
Number of employees	4	170
Administrative staff	1	30
Manual workers	2	130
Managers	1	10
Do overtime	40%	42%
Get annual bonus	100%	80% (not managers)
Permanent staff	25%	70%
Full-time	80%	60%

*1 recession in UK
*2 decline because of new technology

| MARKS | /10 |

Test 4 (Units 13–16)

Vocabulary

1 Circle the correct word to complete these word combinations.

EXAMPLE: waste compost / (disposal)

1 toxic electricity / waste

2 environmental concerns / minutes

3 to hire a consultant / a council

4 reusable finances / resources

5 to clarify a situation / a handbook

6 green policy / polystyrene

7 to win a contract / telemarketing

8 to defuse a crisis / evidence

9 to surf junk mail / the Web

10 raw material / resources

MARKS	/5

2 Use the adjectives to complete the description of the perfect secretary.

~~aggressive~~ attentive confused hostile insulting professional smug welcoming concerned defensive unthreatening

The ideal secretary should be ....

....

....

The ideal secretary shouldn't be *aggressive*...............

....

....

MARKS	/5

3 Write the nouns of the words below in the correct column.

~~concentrate~~ forget propose disturb flexible compete rude explode accept confidential dispose

-ion	concentration
-ity	
-ance	
-al	
-ness	

MARKS	/5

4 Write the instructions for 'Copying text between documents' in the correct order.

Copying text between documents
a Hold down the cursor and highlight the text you want to copy.
b Click on 'file' again and go into your new document.
c Click on 'edit' and 'paste'.
d The text from the first document will appear on your screen.
e Click on 'file' and save the first document.
f Click on 'edit' and 'copy'.

EXAMPLE: ..*a*.. 1 .... 2 .... 3 .... 4 .... 5 ....

MARKS	/5

Grammar and Functions

5 Circle the correct answer to complete the sentences.

EXAMPLE: It's a pity I .... ask you before.

    a don't **(b)** didn't **c** can't

1 I .... have responded to all my e-mails by the end of the day.

    a must **b** will **c** can

2 If I hadn't saved everything onto disk, I .... all my files when the system crashed.

    a would lose **b** lost **c** would have lost

3 It's worth .... the IT department. They should know.

    a to ask **b** to asking **c** asking

4 There's no point .... before nine o'clock because there won't be anyone there.

    a in phoning **b** to phone **c** to phoning

5 It .... have been Simon who rang – he's in Nigeria.

    a shouldn't **b** mustn't **c** can't

MARKS	/5

6 Circle the mistake in each sentence and write the correction.

EXAMPLE: He shouldn't (has) been so rude during the meeting. *have* ....

1 Although working all weekend, I still haven't finished the report. ....

2 I'm really tired. I wish I didn't go to bed so late last night. ....

3 Why doesn't the council recycling more household waste? ....

4 I don't object to pay more money for an environmentally-friendly policy.

....

5 I use the chatlines for informal discussions with colleagues. ....

MARKS	/5

7 Put the words in the correct order, then use the phrases to complete the dialogue below.

a I'll / them / contact.

....

b you / Could / me / give.

....

c tell / me / you / Could
Could you tell me

d waiting / I / mind / four / till / don't.

....

e fault / seem / does / our / This / be / to.

....

f feel / you / I / how / understand.

A: Good morning. Global Phones. Can I help you?

B: Oh hello. I'm phoning about my mobile phone.

A: ...*C*.... exactly what the problem is?

B: Yes. You promised to deliver a replacement mobile phone this morning before twelve but it still hasn't arrived and it's almost two.

A: Oh dear, I am sorry. (1) .... It's so irritating when you wait in for someone and then they don't arrive. (2) ....the reference number, please?

B: Yes, the one I was told yesterday was TY7.

A: Ah yes. Here it is. Let me apologise again. (3)............ . We definitely promised that someone would be with you before midday. (4) .... and phone you back immediately. Can I have your number?

B: Yes, it's 0171 229 7534. (5) .... , but I must leave then.

A: Don't worry, I'll phone you back immediately.

MARKS	/10

Writing

8 You have received these two e-mail messages. Use the notes to write your replies. Each one should be 60–90 words.

```
TO: Holidays of a Lifetime,
INTERNET: holslife@ual.com
FROM: Kim Wickham,
INTERNET: wickham@lloyds.ac.uk
DATE: 13/9   1756
RE: Special offers
I understand that you have some information
about special offers on your Web site but
I'm having problems downloading the
information. Could you e-mail me the Web
site address and let me know when the offers
finish?
Best regards
Kim Wickham
```

Apologise for problems downloading info – ask Website Co-ordinator to look into problem.
Web site address http://www.lifehols.org
Last day of offer: end of this month. USA next month?
Contact again if any more problems / for further information on our full range of holidays.

```
TO: Michael Dumas,
INTERNET: dumas@holslife.ual.com
FROM: Denis Hilton,
INTERNET: hilton@multiling.angel.uk
DATE: 13/9   1203
RE: Social arrangements
Hi!
Are you free on Friday for a film and pizza?
Let me know. Hope all is well.
See you.
Denis
```

Friday no good – meeting Tom for dinner. Saturday? Meet at 6 outside Odeon Leicester Square / see latest James Bond film? Go to Rachel's party?

MARKS	/10

Key

Answers to Test 1

1 *1 mark for each correct answer (10 marks)*
1 despatch 2 attend 3 forward 4 recommend 5 own 6 run
7 train 8 book 9 confirm 10 source

2 *1 mark for each correct answer (5 marks)*
1 climate 2 awful 3 distressing 4 transaction 5 exchange rate

3 *1/2 mark for each correct answer (5 marks)*
1 g 2 e 3 h 4 j 5 a 6 b 7 i 8 d 9 f 10 c

4 *1/2 mark for each correct answer (5 marks)*
1 a 2 a 3 c 4 b 5 b 6 c 7 a 8 b 9 c 10 c

5 *1 mark for each correct answer (5 marks)*
1 to change 2 in 3 of 4 to earn 5 definitely won't

6 *1 mark for each correct answer (10 marks)*
1 A: How about **going** to the cinema **on** Saturday?
  B: Good **idea**.
2 A: I suppose we **could** move the central display unit.
  B: No, I **don't think** it **will / would** work because it's too big.
3 A: Would you mind **waiting** in line?
  B: Oh, I'm sorry. I **didn't realise** there was a queue.
4 A: Are there **any** seats on the next flight to Athens?
  B: Just a moment, Sir. **I'll** check for you.

7 *(10 marks)*
Marking guide
Communication of intention is: 3 good
                               2 satisfactory
                               1 adequate
                               0 very poor
Organisation of ideas is: 2 good
                          1 satisfactory
                          0 poor
Layout, punctuation, spelling is: 2 good
                                  1 satisfactory
                                  0 poor
Accuracy, appropriacy, grammar and vocabulary is: 3 very good
                                                  2 good
                                                  1 adequate
                                                  0 limited

Model answer
FAX
TO: Marie Claire Picot
        Abax Communication
FROM: Jonathan Fox, A B Travel
DATE:
RE: Travel arrangements for Philip Sykes
PAGES: 1 (including this one)

Dear Ms Picot,
Further to your phone call today, I am faxing to confirm the
arrangements for Mr Sykes's forthcoming trip to Seattle.
He is booked on the 0900 BA flight to Seattle from Heathrow Terminal
4 on Tuesday 16 March. He needs to check in at least two hours before
the flight leaves. His arrival time in Seattle will be 1900. I have booked
him into the Sheraton for four nights and the hotel shuttle bus will
meet him at the airport. For his return flight, he is booked on the 0730
flight on Saturday 20 and should arrive back in Heathrow at 0100 on
Sunday 21 March.
Please make sure that he confirms his return flight 48 hours in
advance. The total cost of his flights and accommodation is £755 and I
will send an invoice for this amount tomorrow. The tickets will be with
you by the end of the week.
I hope all these arrangements are satisfactory. Please contact me if I can
be of further assistance.
Yours sincerely,
Jonathan Fox

Answers to Test 2

1 *1/4 mark for each correct answer (5 marks)*
Adjectives: bitter, creamy, fresh, spicy, stale
Shapes: heart-shaped, hexagonal, rectangular, round, triangular
Containers: barrel, carton, jar, sack, tube
Verbs: decorate, fill, fold, pour, coat

2 *1 mark for each correct answer (5 marks)*
1 sales executive
2 assembler
3 ✓
4 distributor
5 sponsor

3 *1/2 mark for each correct answer (5 marks)*
1 innovative 2 inexpensive 3 incredible 4 exclusive
5 individual 6 fantastic 7 pretty 8 terrible 9 powerful
10 damaged

4 *1 mark for each correct answer (5 marks)*
1 screen 2 keyboard 3 modem 4 hard disk 5 guarantee

5 *1 mark for each correct answer (5 marks)*
1 b 2 b 3 c 4 c 5 a

6 *1 mark for each correct answer (5 marks)*
1 considerably higher
2 better and better
3 smells delicious
4 are you doing
5 hard

7 *1/2 mark for each correct word (10 words) (5 marks)*
a 1993–94: Sales **remained** at the same **level**.
b 1994–95: Sales **rose slightly**.
c 1995–96: Sales **fell by** 20000
d 1996–97: The market **expanded dramatically**.
e 1997–98: The market **shrank to** 40000.

8 *1 mark for each correct answer (5 marks)*
1 I've got an appointment with
2 Could I take your name, please?
3 Which company are you from?
4 I'll tell him you're here.
5 Can I take your coat?

9 *(10 marks)*
See marking guide in Test 1.

Model answer
Ms P Hughes   Communications Express
Office Recruitment   95 The Broadway
Napier House   London W13 0RT
56–59 Edison Street   *Date*
London WC1 9JK

Dear Ms Hughes

Thank you for your enquiry about Communications Express
products. I enclose information on our full range of products
including our fax machines.
I am also enclosing product sheets for the Alpha 768 and Alpha 945
which are new this year. The product sheets include all the
specifications for the machines.
If you would like to receive more information, please do not hesitate
to contact me at the above address and I will be delighted to send you
more details. You might also find it useful if I visited your office to
demonstrate how both machines work. I look forward to hearing
from you.

Yours sincerely
Anthony Thompson

Senior Sales Executive
Communications Express

Answers to Test 3

1 *½ mark for each correct answer (5 marks)*
1 i 2 e 3 d 4 h 5 b 6 j 7 g 8 a 9 c 10 f

2 *½ mark for each correct answer (2½ marks)*
1 enthusiastic 2 sensitive 3 fashionable 4 thoughtful
5 wealthy

3 *¼ mark for each correct answer (2½ marks)*
TV programmes: sitcom, drama, soap opera, comedy
people: viewer, audience, correspondent
things to read: script, wire, autocue

4 *1 mark for each correct phrasal verb and 1 for each correct synonym*
(10 marks)
1 go ahead (start) 2 put forward (suggest) 3 talk over (discuss)
4 tuned in (listen) 5 draw up (write)

5 *1 mark for each correct answer (5 marks)*
1 c 2 a 3 b 4 a 5 c

6 *1 mark for each correct answer (5 marks)*
1 He's **been** working for MTV for six months.
2 I always listen to the seven o'clock news. So **do** I!
3 To put **it** another way, I think we should carry out some research.
4 When I started my present job, I **had** never used a database system
before.
5 They told me **to** be diplomatic.

7 *1 mark for each correct answer (10 marks)*
1 background in 2 experience of 3 been working 4 interested
5 familiar 6 prefer 7 like it the best 8 capable 9 can't stand
10 rather

8 *(10 marks)*
See marking guide in Test 1.

Model answer
As you will see from the graph I am enclosing with this report, the
number of people employed by Lewis Electronics has increased
dramatically since the company was set up in 1980, from 4 to 170.
There was a steady increase in the size of the workforce in the first
half of the 1980s and then a sharp decrease during the UK recession.
However, since 1990, the workforce has increased steadily although
there has been a gradual decrease since 1995 with the introduction of
new technology.
Although far more staff are now employed on a permanent basis, a
higher percentage choose to work part-time. Another change is that
whereas all employees received an annual bonus when the company
first opened, a lower percentage receive one now. Finally, one area
where there has been little change is in the amount of overtime that
Lewis employees do. This is an area that should be looked at, as
overtime payments cost the company a lot of money each year.

Answers to Test 4

1 *½ mark for each correct answer (5 marks)*
1 waste 2 concerns 3 a consultant 4 resources 5 a situation
6 policy 7 a contract 8 a crisis 9 the Web 10 material

2 *½ mark for each correct answer (5 marks)*
The ideal secretary should be attentive, professional, welcoming,
concerned, unthreatening.
The ideal secretary shouldn't be confused, hostile, insulting, smug,
defensive.

3 *½ mark for each correct answer (5 marks)*
-ion: explosion, competition
-ity: flexibility, confidentiality
-ance: acceptance, disturbance
-al: disposal, proposal
-ness: forgetfulness, rudeness

4 *1 mark for each correct answer (5 marks)*
1 f 2 e 3 b 4 c 5 d

5 *1 mark for each correct answer (5 marks)*
1 b 2 c 3 c 4 a 5 c

6 *1 mark for each correct answer (5 marks)*
1 In spite of / despite
2 hadn't gone
3 recycle
4 paying
5 I use chatlines

7 *2 marks for each correct answer (10 marks)*
1(f) I understand how you feel.
2(b) Could you give me the reference number, please?
3(e) This does seem to be our fault.
4(a) I'll contact them and phone you back immediately.
5(d) I don't mind waiting till four, but I must leave then.

8 *(10 marks)*
See marking guide in Test 1.
Model answer
1 TO: Kim Wickham, INTERNET: wickham@lloyds.ac.uk
FROM: Michael Dumas, Holidays of a Lifetime,
INTERNET: holslife@ual.com
DATE: 14/9   0930
RE: Special offers: reply
Dear Ms Wickham.
Thank you for your e-mail and interest in our holidays. I am sorry
that you've had problems downloading information from our Web
site: I have asked our Web site Co-ordinator to look into this. Our
Web site address is http://www.lifehols.org
The special offers finish at the end of this month but we hope to be
able to offer ones to the USA next month. Please let me know if you
have any more problems accessing our Web site and if I can give any
further information on our full range of holidays.
Regards,
Michael Dumas.

2 TO: Denis Hilton, INTERNET: hilton@multiling.angel.uk
FROM: Michael Dumas, INTERNET: dumas@holslife.ual.com
DATE: 13/9   1443
RE: Social arrangements: reply
Thanks for the e-mail. I'm afraid that Friday isn't any good for me as
I'm meeting Tom for dinner. But what about Saturday? We could
meet outside the Odeon Leicester Square at 6 – the latest James Bond
film is on there, and I'd really like to see it. We could go on to
Rachel's party? Let me know.
Best wishes. Michael